Buckingham at 25

Buckingham at 25

Freeing the Universities from State Control

Edited by
JAMES TOOLEY

iea

The Institute of Economic Affairs

First published in Great Britain in 2001 by
The Institute of Economic Affairs
2 Lord North Street
Westminster
London SW1P 3LB
in association with Profile Books Ltd

A CIP catalogue record for this book is available from the British Library.

ISBN 0 255 36512 8

Many IEA publications are translated into languages other than English or are
reprinted. Permission to translate or to reprint should be sought from the
General Director at the address above.

Typeset in Stone by MacGuru
info@macguru.org.uk

Printed and bound in Great Britain by Hobbs the Printers

CONTENTS

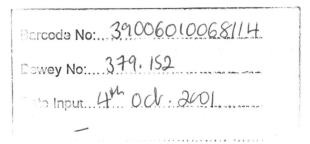

THE AUTHORS

James Tooley

James Tooley is Professor of Education Policy at the University of Newcastle-upon-Tyne. Prior to this he was Senior Research Fellow in the School of Education, University of Manchester. He is also Director of the Education Programme at the Institute of Economic Affairs, London. Professor Tooley gained his PhD from the Institute of Education, University of London and has held research positions at the University of Oxford's Department of Educational Studies and the National Foundation for Educational Research. He has taught at Simon Fraser University (Canada), the University of the Western Cape (South Africa) and as a mathematics teacher at schools in Zimbabwe. He is a columnist for *Economic Affairs*, and is the author of *Disestablishing the School* (1995), *Education without the State* (1996), *The Higher Education Debate* (1997), *Educational Research: A Critique* (with Doug Darby, 1998), *The Global Education Industry* (1999) and *Reclaiming Education* (2000).

Sir Alan Peacock

Sir Alan Peacock, now 79, retired in 1985 from his last full-time academic post as the first Vice-Chancellor of the University of Buckingham. Previously he held chairs of economics at Edinburgh

(1957–62) and York (1962–78) and was for three years (1973–76) full-time Chief Economic Adviser at the Department of Trade and Industry with the rank of Deputy Secretary. He co-founded the David Hume Institute, Edinburgh, and was its first Executive Director (1985–91), during which period he was Chairman of the Home Office Committee on the Financing of the BBC, which reported in 1986. He is still 'enjoyably busy' writing in diverse fields such as public choice analysis, the economics of the welfare state, the economics of civil justice and, unusually, the economics of the arts – he chaired the Scottish Arts Council from 1986 to 1992. He is a Fellow of the British Academy, of the Royal Society of Edinburgh, and of the Italian National Academy, and has been awarded eleven honorary degrees. His latest publications are *Public Choice Analysis in Historical Perspective* (Cambridge, 1992), *Paying the Piper: Culture, Music and Money* (EUP, 1993), *The Political Economy of Economic Freedom* (Elgar, 1997), and (with Brian Main) *What Price Civil Justice?* (IEA Hobart Paper 139, 2000).

Sir Graham Hills

Professor Sir Graham Hills was educated at London University, reading and researching chemistry at Birkbeck College. He taught at Imperial College for ten years before being appointed Professor of Chemistry at Southampton University. In between he was a visiting professor in Canada, the United States and Argentina. In 1980 he was appointed Principal and Vice-Chancellor at the University of Strathclyde in Glasgow. During this time he was Scottish Governor of the BBC (1988–93) and a member of the Prime Minister's Advisory Council on Science and Technology (1986–94). He is the founding father of the prospective University of the Highlands and Islands of Scotland.

Baroness Warwick of Undercliffe

Diana Warwick was appointed Chief Executive of the Committee of Vice-Chancellors and Principals in 1995 (now Universities UK). Universities UK is the 'voice of UK universities' that represents their executive heads. Previously she had been Chief Executive of the Westminster Foundation for Democracy, which was established by Parliament to provide funding to organisations involved in strengthening democratic development overseas. During the 1980s she was the General Secretary of the Association of University Teachers, representing some 30,000 academic and senior staff in UK universities.

Diana was a member of the Employment Appeals Tribunal from 1984 until 1999, and the Standing Committee on Standards in Public Life (Nolan/Neill Committee) from 1994 until 1999. From 1985 until 1995 she served as a board member of the British Council, was a governor of the Commonwealth Institute until 1995, and a member of the TUC General Council between 1989 and 1992.

She has been a member of the Executive Council of the Industrial Society since 1987, Chairperson of Voluntary Service Overseas (VSO) since 1994, and a trustee of St Catherine's Foundation, Windsor, since 1996. She is a member of the Technology Foresight Steering Group and the House of Lords Select Committee on Science and Technology.

Diana was born in Bradford, Yorkshire, and graduated from Bedford College, University of London, in 1967 with an honours degree in Sociology and Economics. She has been awarded honorary degrees by Bradford University and the Open University. She was made a life peer in July 1999.

Kenneth Minogue

Kenneth Minogue is Emeritus Professor of Political Science at the London School of Economics and Political Science. He was born in New Zealand, educated in Australia, and is the author of *The Liberal Mind*, *Nationalism*, *The Concept of a University*, and *Alien Powers: The Pure Theory of Ideology*, as well as academic essays on a great range of problems in political theory. In his academic persona he has lectured at universities and research institutes in the United States, the Netherlands, Australia and many other countries, and has also written columns for *The Times* and the *Times Higher Education Supplement* and reviews in both intellectual and academic journals. In 1986 he presented a six-part television programme on free-market economics called *The New Enlightenment*, repeated in 1988. A frequent commentator for radio and television on European Community issues, he was Chairman of the Bruges Group from 1991 until 1993. He is a director of the Centre for Policy Studies, for which he has written 'The Egalitarian Conceit' and 'The Constitutional Mania'.

Tony Dickson

Tony Dickson is currently Deputy Vice-Chancellor (Academic) at Northumbria University, where his responsibilities include academic policy, academic programmes, international development, and e-business capability. He has previously held academic posts at Paisley University and Glasgow Caledonian, where he was head of the Department of Sociology and Dean of the Faculty of Life and Social Sciences. Major publications include *Scottish Capitalism* and *The Politics of Industrial Closure*. Interests include corporate strategy and e-business models.

Jacob van Lutsenburg Maas

Jack Maas recently completed a 27-year career with the World Bank Group. He joined the Education Department of the World Bank in January 1974. After participating in various policy-making activities, he transferred into education lending operations, first in the Eastern Africa Region of the Bank, then in the East Asia and the Pacific Region, before becoming Chief of the Education Unit for the Latin America and Caribbean Region in 1988. In 1992 he became Chief of the Population and Human Resource Development Division of the Bank's East Africa Department, and in 1996 Lead Education Specialist for the Bank's Africa Region.

In 1997 the World Bank seconded Mr Maas to the International Finance Corporation, the arm of the World Bank Group that provides financial services for investment projects in developing countries which are sponsored by the private sector. The purpose of his secondment was to assist IFC in determining if investing in education enterprises in developing countries could become a viable and new product line. He transferred to IFC a year later when it was decided to begin implementation of this new direction, leading to the creation of a new Health and Education Group in IFC in April 2000. He retired from IFC in March 2001 and is now a consultant in the emerging global education marketplace.

Prior to his career in the World Bank Group, Mr Maas taught

in public schools in Ohio and New Jersey in the early 1960s and trained teachers in Uganda in the mid-1960s under the auspices of the United States Agency for International Development and Uganda's Ministry of Education. He was lecturer in the Socio-Economic Aspects of Education at Makerere University, Uganda, for two years in the early 1970s and obtained his PhD in Comparative Education and Sociology from Teachers College, Columbia University, in 1975.

David Halpern

David Halpern is a lecturer at the Faculty of Social and Political Sciences, University of Cambridge. He was formerly a director of the centre-left think tank Nexus, and a research fellow at Nuffield College, Oxford, the Center for European Studies at Harvard, and the Policy Studies Institute, London.

Duke Maskell

An ex-university English lecturer, Duke Maskell runs, with Ian Robinson, a small publisher, Edgeways Books, specialising in literary and social criticism. They are the publishers of *The* Real *Common Worship*, an attack on the Church of England's latest replacement for the Book of Common Prayer. He is joint author (with Ian Robinson) of *The New Idea of a University*, published by Haven Books, Burbage House, 83 Curtain Road, London, EC2A 3BS, which argues that the new mass university, promoted as an investment, is not only not an investment but not a university either. Their radical suggestion is that the very new idea of a university, as a place where masses of people are trained in supposedly economically valuable skills, should be replaced by the very old idea of somewhere a few receive a liberal education: our idea of a university should come from J. H. Newman, Jane Austen and Socrates, not from ministers or civil servants.

Niall Ferguson

Niall Ferguson is Professor of Political and Financial History at the University of Oxford and Director of the Internet-based company Boxmind. He has published works on nineteenth- and twentieth-century European political and financial history, notably the prize-winning history of the Rothschilds bank, *The World's Banker*, and the best-selling history of the First World War, *The Pity of War*. His latest publication, *The Cash Nexus: Money and Power in the Modern World*, was published by Penguin in February 2001. Although he continues to take a special interest in German history (especially the period 1870–1945), he has also published essays on counterfactual history. He is currently working on a history of European monarchy in the nineteenth century.

John Clarke

Before coming to Buckingham, Professor Clarke spent a number of years at Oxford. He read history at Wadham College and graduated with first-class honours. He was then elected to a Prize Fellowship at All Souls College. In the early 1970s, he completed his doctorate on social and economic history in the early nineteenth century. Professor Clarke has published books on *George III* (1972), *England in the Age of Cobbett* (1977), *British Diplomacy and Foreign Policy* (1989), as well as others on local history. As a person whose family has lived in the area for generations (his great-grandfather was a village blacksmith at Lillingston Dayrell), his work on the history of the towns of Brackley and Buckingham has been greatly appreciated by the local community. Professor Clarke has been associated with the University of Buckingham and its predecessor, the University College at Buckingham, from the start of the project in 1976. He was Dean of Admissions and Senior Lecturer in History. In the latter capacity he helped to set up the degree programme in History, Politics and English Literature, and later the single honours programmes in history and English. He became Professor of History in 1999. John Clarke has taught undergraduates at Wadham, Brasenose, Worcester, Balliol, St Hugh's and St John's Colleges in Oxford and has also supervised the work of several graduate students.

Norman Barry

Norman Barry is a political theorist with an interest in political economy and in the connections between politics, ethics and economics. A graduate of the University of Exeter, he lectured in politics at Queen's University, Belfast, and at Birmingham Polytechnic (now the University of Central England) before being appointed as a Reader in Politics at the University of Buckingham in 1982. His books include *Hayek's Social and Economic Philosophy* (1979), *An Introduction to Modern Political Theory* (1981), *The Morality of Business Enterprise* (1991), *Classical Liberalism in the Age of Post-Communism* (1996) and *Business Ethics* (1998). He was awarded a chair in Social and Political Theory at Buckingham in 1984. He has been a visitng scholar at the Center for Social Philosophy and Policy, Bowling Green State University, Ohio, and at the Liberty Fund,

Indianapolis. He is a member of the Advisory Councils of the Institute of Economic Affairs, London; the Institute for the Study of Civil Society, London; and the David Hume Institute, Edinburgh.

Terence Kealey

Terence Kealey graduated in medicine from St Bartholomew's Hospital Medical School, London University, in 1975. He then specialised in biomedical research, obtaining his DPhil from the Department of Clinical Biochemistry, Oxford University, in 1982. After an MRC Training Fellowship and a Wellcome Senior Clinical Research Fellowship, he settled in 1986 in Cambridge as a university lecturer and NHS consultant in clinical biochemistry. In 2001 he was appointed Vice-Chancellor of the University of Buckingham. In his biomedical research he has focused on the cell biology of human skin. But Terence Kealey has also studied the economics of science and higher education. His 1996 book *The Economic Laws of Scientific Research* argues that, contrary to myth, there is no market failure in science, and that it can be entrusted safely to the free market.

FOREWORD

Twenty-five years ago a small group of far-sighted people founded what is now the University of Buckingham. They did this because they saw government control steadily encircling all our other universities, dependent as they are on state funding. Knowing that government control is the enemy of freedom, they were determined to establish one that was truly independent.

Against the odds, they succeeded. We should salute them. Buckingham has flourished, and it remains the only UK university which is independent of government. It is vital that it continue to develop successfully. All those who cherish freedom need to play their part to ensure this.

State control of universities is damaging to standards, as nationalisation of any other activity has always proved. Furthermore, history shows that when governments control universities, even if they do not intend this, they stifle freedom and endanger liberty in a fundamental way.

In Germany, state control of universities became virtually total after the inflation of the 1920s wiped out their investments, and they then became dependent on government funding. They became corrupted. The majority of holders of university chairs had already joined the Nazi Party voluntarily before 1933. Opposition to the Nazi regime, which any oasis of freedom ought to have fostered, was almost non-existent. The First Supplemental Decree forced the retirement of all non-Aryan academic staff by law in November 1935; but such was the acceptance of state domination that most of the harm had already been done.

It may seem far-fetched to compare pre-war Germany with our situation today. However, history shows that there is a powerful connection between dependence on public money, with the constant thirst for more of it, on the one hand, and the propensity to suppress opposition to government thinking on the other. Public money corrupts the pursuit of truth.

Freedom of thought can only truly flourish at institutions which are free and independent; it cannot do so if fettered by government interference. Moreover, an independent university must respond to its 'market'. It should be responsible to those it serves, not to government diktat. If it does not provide the standards of excellence which its students expect, it deserves not to succeed. If the quality of its research proves fruitless, it will wither. Universities serving their 'markets' with excellence are the ones that flourish. This requires the free pursuit of truth in teaching and research.

Public-sector universities in the UK will now have to tell the Treasury where research spending is going. Does anyone think government officials would have sanctioned the work of Faraday or Darwin? We should remember Galileo's capitulation when Pope Urban showed him the instruments of torture. He won through in the end, but only in the face of government attempts to stop him in his pursuit of truth.

Adam Smith was teaching at Glasgow University 250 years ago, and students then paid teachers whose lectures they attended directly. When the University offered him a salary to recognise his fame and success, he declined the offer, so strong was his belief in market principles. He had seen how inferior Oxford and Cambridge had become at that time, compared to the Scottish universities, and he attributed this to the fact that their academics enjoyed guaranteed salaries, which the Scottish universities could not afford; in Scotland they had to respond to their 'market'.

State funding, on which our universities depend, began after World War II, and the desirability of it has never since been seriously questioned; never, that is, until the founding of Buckingham 25 years ago. In recent years, sadly, the growth of bureaucratic control, which accompanies state funding, has been accelerating. The Dearing Report has made the problem more acute, with its accentuation of vocational orientation at the expense of the true university purpose of a liberal education. According to Dearing, teachers in universities are going to have to be licensed by a new government body, an Institute of Learning and Teaching in Higher Education. This is to be a new monopoly qualification, a near state control; it will prove to be, unfortunately, a hurdle, excluding outstanding brains who will have none of this kind of authoritarian approach. Can anyone imagine Einstein, Karl Popper or Wittgenstein going for an ILTHE qualification?

Today, the University of Buckingham stands alone. The safety of faculty jobs is dependent on the judgement of the 'market' Buckingham is serving; it is not dependent on the 'measurements of output' judged by controlling bureaucrats. In the US, publicly funded universities have to work by reference to benchmarks set by those funded by the private sector, and those include, as everyone knows, some of the finest universities in the world. In just the same way, we in the UK need a first-class, privately funded university, independent of government control. This is why the University of Buckingham must continue to flourish.

SIR MARTIN JACOMB
Chancellor of the University of Buckingham

INTRODUCTION
THE FUTURE OF HIGHER EDUCATION IN THE UK: SEVEN STRAWS IN THE WIND
James Tooley

In the year of the Silver Jubilee of the University of Buckingham, it is time to take stock. It is commonplace now for commentators to note that universities are in crisis – in terms of funding and resources and, above all, staff morale. Some new way has to be found for them to flourish and prosper. A useful way of locating this 'new' way involves relearning the lessons that led to the creation of a truly independent university – Buckingham – in the first place, and reapplying these to the changing conditions of the present. To this end, the Institute of Economic Affairs is marking the 25th anniversary by republishing Harry S. Ferns' *Towards an Independent University*, first published in 1969, which provided the intellectual framework for the creation of Buckingham as a university (see pp 249–93). This is complemented with a selection of essays by notable academics and commentators, all specially commissioned for this volume, reflecting on the history of Buckingham in particular, and the past, present and future of universities in general.

In this introductory essay, I set out what I see as 'seven straws in the wind' which are likely to bring change to higher education, putting these into the context of the reasons why Harry S. Ferns believed that there should be an 'independent' university.

Before outlining what these are, it is important to clear up one issue. People talk loosely about 'state', 'public' or 'government' universities in Britain, and contrast these with the only 'private' university here, that is, Buckingham. However, it is the case that, technically, *all* universities in the UK are private institutions. They were either created as such by their Royal Charters, or by statute (including the 1992 Education Act which converted the old polytechnics into universities). Some of them, including the London School of Economics, are even companies limited by guarantee.

If pushed on this issue (and I've pushed many, including a former Chairman of the Committee of Vice-Chancellors and Principals, CVCP, now Universities UK), many will fall back on the statement that 'what they meant' was that universities are effectively 'public' institutions because of their dependence on public funding and their close regulation by government.

In terms of regulations, certainly, people are on the strongest ground. Among the panoply of regulations that universities come under, there is the detailed assessment of teaching by the QAA – the Quality Assurance Agency – and the painstaking monitoring of research through the RAE – the Research Assessment Exercise.

However, in terms of government funding, the situation is not quite as stark as many people might imagine. The latest figures on the Higher Education Funding Council for England (HEFCE) website[1] show that in total less than three-fifths of funding (some 57.4 per cent) currently comes from central and local government, while the remaining two-fifths comes from a variety of private sources, including overseas student fees (some of which may, of course, be provided by overseas governments), UK charities and

---

1   HEFCE, April 1998, 'Private Investment in Higher Education', www.hefce.ac.uk/pubs/hefce/1998/98_18.htm.

other private research bodies. These are total figures: a few British universities require only 20 per cent or less of government funding in order to prosper and thrive.

Indeed, university dependence on state funding is not as pronounced as even these figures suggest. Only 41 per cent of university funding comes as a direct government grant (from HEFCE). A further 12 per cent comes via local education authorities (LEAs) for student fees, and hence is already coming via some sort of market or 'voucher' mechanism – students themselves, by and large, choose where to attend university, and the LEA funds follow them to the university of their choice. And there is 5 per cent or so of funds from Research Councils which are also, to a great extent, the outcome of competition among researchers or research teams for these funds.

What this discussion suggests is that we need to be very careful when we think of the future options for British universities. They already are private institutions, and the fact that they have conceded their autonomy and independence for the sake of the *direct* funding that makes up only a *minority* of their total income should not blind us to this fact, nor to the potential behind it.

With this as background, what are the seven straws in the wind that I think signal the way things will change in the future, and how do these connect with Harry Ferns' ideas?

The first is the way in which some of the more prestigious universities are currently rebelling against government regulation. The London School of Economics (LSE) is leading the revolt. In March this year, it resolved to break away from the QAA process. Its board passed a motion arguing that the QAA 'has infringed academic freedom, imposed its own bureaucratic and pedagogical agenda, neglected student "intellectual development" and used incompetent and unprofessional reviewers'.[2] In its place, the LSE is looking to develop with the Russell Group – the élite group of British universities – an alternative quality assurance system. The QAA approach, its motion continued, is 'an insult to the Russell Group'. In a similar vein, a few days earlier, King's College London had 'disowned' its QAA report, declaring that the agency had failed to 'intellectually engage' with the university. All this signals a growing dissatisfaction with government regulation, and a willingness to look to alternative, private means of self-regulation. Harry Ferns had some prescient things to say about regulation, and a view of the way forward. He asks: 'how can we tell whether an university is any good or not?' (p. 271–72). He goes on: 'The real test is whether or not students want to enter it and how much they and their parents are willing to sacrifice in the effort to do so. At the moment some universities are probably better than other universities, but there is no means of knowing ... If every university had to stand on its own feet, there would be no need for the Auditor General to crawl around the premises seeing how the money is being spent while assuring everyone that he is not interested in policy.'

Since he wrote that, much has changed, of course. Now the universities don't have the 'Auditor General' 'crawling' around, 'not interested in policy'. Now the universities are under a much more extensive and intrusive inspection regime, one that most explicitly *is* concerned with policy. And it is this regime that some of the most prestigious universities are rebelling against. Ferns didn't put forward an alternative private regulatory system as a way for-

---

2 'Universities sinking under inspection load', *Times Higher Education Supplement*, 23 March 2001 (www.thesis.co.uk/search/story.asp?id=71795&state_value=archive).

ward, mentioning only the market mechanism of demand. But the route suggested by the LSE and King's College is perfectly consistent with these ideas, and our first straw in the wind for changes that will transform the current system.

Harry Ferns did recognise the one big obstacle to getting Buckingham started – 'nearly all students who can gain admission to the state-supported system will continue to prefer the existing universities' (p. 272), if these are free at the point of entry and the truly independent university is not. This aspect of the lack of level playing field brings us to the second straw in the wind: In England and Wales (although not now in Scotland) we have finally crossed the Rubicon concerning the charging of student fees. It took New Labour to do it, and admittedly the fees charged for students are rather low: at about £1,000 per annum making up no more than 20 per cent of the real costs of courses, and in many cases considerably less. Many students, too, have free or subsidised places. Nevertheless, the principle has been conceded, and now several universities are exploring the possibility of charging top-up fees, or more realistic fees. Indeed, given that Buckingham degrees take two years instead of three, the opportunity costs are less, and it may not be long before it can compete on a completely level playing field with the state funded universities.

But shouldn't everyone have access to higher education, even those who cannot afford the fees? This brings us to the third straw in the wind, the existence worldwide of commercially oriented student loan programmes that can ease access for those who can't currently afford higher education, but whose *future* enhanced income would make expenditure *now* completely viable. Indeed, Harry Ferns – again showing prescience – points to some of the possibilities: 'Methods of pre-payment of fees by life assurance (with assistance of income-tax rebates) and "post-payment" by species of hire purchase' (p. 273); he goes on to outline a model of hire purchase that would be suitable for Buckingham.

There are some particularly interesting loan models being developed around the world that could inform the current debate here – and one of the models is discussed by Jack Maas in his chapter below looking at the work of the International Finance Corporation in helping to finance private education projects, including student loans. Another is that created in 1995 by INSEAD, one of the leading business schools in Europe, an offshoot of Harvard Business School – a model that has since been imitated by other commercial banks. Although poor students from eastern and central Europe couldn't finance themselves from their *current* income, it was realised that there was a great chance they could do so from *future* earnings.

Joining forces with the European Bank of Reconstruction and Development (EBRD), the concept of the MBA student loan programme was created. Other top-tiered schools have since joined in the programme, including IESE in Barcelona, the London Business School, the University of Michigan, and the Business School of Rotterdam, Erasmus. The principle is that a cash cushion is needed by the lender. To accomplish this, it asks students to borrow a 'little bit more' than their fees, and the schools to accept 'a little bit less'. Whatever is left is put into the 'School Trust Account', to be used to finance defaults.

Why would a student agree to borrow a 'little bit more'? (After all, they have to pay interest on it.) The students accept the concept of 'cross-insurance' with their colleagues within their MBA programmes. Why would the school agree to give a discount? The most clever twist in the scheme is that the college can use the entire contribution to the School Trust Fund for scholarships (and hence for fee income) once the loans are repaid. This brings a huge incentive to the colleges to bring psychological pressure to bear on students not to default. Indeed, in its first pilot phase all students repaid their loans.

So suppose a course levied a tuition fee of $10,000. The student borrows $10,750, and the college is persuaded to accept $9,250 instead of the full fee. The difference – $1,500 – is put into the trust fund, to be used to finance defaulters. Repayment of the student loan then takes place over a period of up to 13.5 years, and there is no need for collateral or co-signature. From a purely banking perspective, the long maturity of this loan is for marketing reasons. Students who take out the loans don't have much money. They would be put off by a high monthly repayment. However, the MBA transforms their opportunities, and it has been the Bank's experience that people pay back the loan in a much shorter timescale than the 13.5 years allowed.

This type of loan scheme points to the possibility that similar schemes could be devised in this country, allowing increased access for the poorest in society, while still ensuring that the universities themselves get adequate funding.

Mention of the experience of other countries brings us to the fourth straw in the wind: the growth of private universities worldwide. They are showing that governments are not needed to provide or to fund higher education, and that the private sector is ready and waiting to pick up the slack, if given a chance. They provide lessons that should make us sit up and think about the possibility of increasing private-sector funding here too.

I've seen this growth of private education at first hand, in some of the most unlikely places. In China in 1998 there were 1,236 private universities (54 per cent of the total number of universities)[3] only fifteen years after private education had been made legal. In Somaliland, the republic that has broken away from war-torn Somalia, two private universities have recently emerged, Amoud University in Borama and the University of Hargeisa in the capital, funded more or less entirely from private sources, including student fees. The primitive state could not hope to fund or develop higher education there, but the private sector has stepped in to fill the void.

Ferns argued that an independent university in Britain would act as a demonstration that 'people on their own can meet a community need with no assistance from the state ... Such an act of initiative and free co-operation among individuals will energise the community as a whole' (p. 259–260). He would be pleased to know that such a spirit of educational self-help is alive and well in many developing countries, and is revitalising the communities as he predicted.

Many of these private universities across the world are traditional, not-for-profit universities, as is the University of Buckingham. There is nothing wrong with that. However, in *Towards an Independent University* Ferns did wonder whether we had got it wrong about higher education's need for subsidy. While Buckingham required a substantial capital sum of about £5 million to get started, he argued that 'there is no reason why the foundation funds should not be repayable over, say, 50 years, should not bear interest and should not be secured on land and buildings'. Indeed,

3   Official statistics provided by Professor Wu Wei, Vice-Chairman, China Educational Science Association, and Ye Zhihing, Chief, Division of Educational Philosophy, National Centre for Education Development Research, Ministry of Education, 21 July 1999, Beijing.

he insisted, to 'suppose otherwise is to pander to the false notion that education is a special kind of activity dependent on charitable impulses or state subsidies' (p. 280).

Ferns' comments are very interesting given the fifth straw in the wind – the rise of the *for-profit* university globally. In countries such as Brazil and South Africa, as I've reported elsewhere,[4] there are chains of private universities such as Objetivo/UNIP and Midrand developing, often expanding on a franchise basis. In the USA, too, there are several such chains, including DeVry, the University of Phoenix and Sylvan Learning Systems.

DeVry, for instance, has 21 campuses across the USA and Canada, serving 47,000 students, offering general education integrated into specialised curricula in accounting, business, computers, electronics, information technology, technical management and telecommunications management. DeVry courses are accredited by the Higher Learning Commission, listed by the US Department of Education as a recognised accrediting institution.

A key feature of these for-profit chains is that they are hungry for international expansion, and have the investment to match their desires. At the forefront of this international expansion is Sylvan. It began moving into the higher education business by buying a controlling stake in Universidad Europea de Madrid, Spain's largest for-profit university. The university has a capacity for 10,000 students and average tuition fees of about £4,700 per year. From there, after setting up its Sylvan International Universities division, the company moved to take a 80 per cent controlling interest in the Universidad del Valle in Mexico, with 32,000 full-time students in fourteen campuses. The third university it

4   See Tooley, James (1999), *The Global Education Industry*, IEA/IFC, London.

acquired was Universidad de las Americas, a 5,500-student private university in Santiago, Chile. It has also acquired the 1,000-student Les Roches Hotel Management School in Switzerland.

Sylvan does not intend to grow in the USA, where it sees the market as already saturated, but seeks its expansion in Latin America and Europe, buying controlling stakes in existing private universities, introducing major investments in expansion and upgrading of facilities and curriculum support, and putting in place a common institutional management framework. As part of its major investment programme, already the Universidad Europea has been transformed into Europe's first 'wireless' campus, where students, faculty and staff are able to access coursework and administrative and research services via the Internet, 'any time, anywhere' on campus, using wireless laptop computers.

Sylvan will also begin to offer its varied curricula to each of its universities, to truly begin to globalise its university network, through distance learning. And this brings us to the sixth straw in the wind, the rise of 'borderless' education – that is, education delivered by a provider in a different country from where the learning takes place. Many of the major universities are taking advantage of the opportunities offered here. For instance, Oxford University has signed a deal with Princeton, Yale and Stanford universities in the USA to create a new 'virtual college', the 'University Alliance for Life-Long Learning'. First targeting the universities' half a million alumni, but later offering courses to others, the alliance will offer students the chance to keep up to date with research and teaching, through live video and Internet links. Similarly, Cambridge University's Judge Institute of Management has joined with FT Knowledge to launch an executive on-line MBA. There is an explosion of such courses in the USA – enabling students to access courses anywhere in the world.

And of course it is not just the traditional universities that are moving into this area. The Apollo Group, featured in an edition of *Economic Affairs*,[5] which already has about 90,000 adult part-time students at its 32 campuses and 71 learning centres of the University of Phoenix, is now offering on-line courses anywhere in the world. Masters-level courses in subjects from Education to Technology Management, Accounting to Nursing Studies, all accredited by the Higher Learning Commission in the USA, are being offered as 100 per cent on-line degrees.

All of this points to an increasingly competitive global market for higher education; universities here will have to at least take cognisance of these new competitive pressures. Harry Ferns wanted the University of Buckingham to be at the forefront of this revolution too: he didn't think the new university should worry about mass education: 'Modern media of communication will enable a small number of brilliant teachers to reach more students more often than any do at present' (p. 277), and this was something that he very much applauded.

Which brings us to the seventh, and final, straw in the wind. This is the on-going debate here about the future of the universities – of which the articles brought together in this celebratory volume are a significant contribution. Here we have discussions from a range of perspectives and ideological standpoints, each sharing a willingness to 'think the unthinkable' about the future of universities in ways that would have been impossible to contemplate even five years ago. The fact that the debate is happening now in this way augurs well, I believe, for the future of higher education.

---

5 See Sperling, John (1998), 'The American for-profit university: a model for the information economy', *Economic Affairs*, 18, 3, 11–16.

First, we have Sir Alan Peacock, in a revised lecture delivered to celebrate the University of Buckingham's 25th anniversary. He wonders whether universities are necessary any more. Interestingly, this is not just from the perspective that there are changes taking place. He also points back to the wisdom of Adam Smith, who commented in *The Wealth of Nations*: 'When a man has learnt his lesson very well, it surely can be of little importance where or from whom he learnt it.'

Sir Graham Hills then sets out a trenchant critique of the way British universities arrived at their state of 'abject ... financial dependence on central government'. But he is optimistic about the future if universities embrace a simple financial reform that requires them to charge student market fees, and if they can capitalise on the power of the internet to reduce their costs and experiment with alternative approaches to learning.

Sir Graham is not particularly flattering about the Committee of Vice Chancellors and Principals, now Universities UK, having been appointed as one of their number in 1980; Baroness Warwick, Chief Executive of Universities UK, puts forward their case. She points out that, while universities receive substantial government funding, there is a 'fine balancing act' to be performed between 'freedom and accountability'. Too much accountability, she says, and government will end up stifling innovation and entrepreneurship. At present, she says, this 'crucial balancing act has not yet been achieved'.

Her contribution is followed by Kenneth Minogue's robust demonstration of the 'collapse' of the academic in Britain. Professor Minogue outlines how the mission of universities has become subordinated to 'the priorities of the state', which has 'destroyed the reflective quality' of academic life. There is a solution however:

what is needed is to 'leave universities alone', allowing them to flourish independently of government.

Addressing the twin issues of accountability and funding, Professor Tony Dickson wonders whether the relation between the universities and the state is 'A Faustian Bargain?' He questions the current 'heavy reliance on public funding' as being undesirable, and suggests that more thoroughgoing privatisation – in terms of much greater private investment and more realistic student fees – is the way forward for British universities.

Jack Maas's contribution provides an important international perspective on the growth of the private higher education sector in developing countries. Jack Maas was for many years the Lead Education Specialist at the International Finance Corporation, the private finance arm of the World Bank, and instrumental in formulating the Bank's interest in investment in private education as a way of promoting equitable development. He outlines the progress so far, pointing to the variety of opportunities for investment globally, and discusses implications for the future.

Two contributions then probe in detail the issue of 'Who should pay for HE?' Dr David Halpern argues that a 'who benefit pays' principle 'is a useful guide to funding reform', pointing to the need for students to contribute a 'substantial proportion of the costs of their higher education'. Halpern, however, believes that 'universities should receive grants from government in so far as their work contributes to the public good.' This issue is taken up by Duke Maskell, a former university lecturer and author of the recent iconoclastic *The New Idea of a University*. In his incisive polemic, Maskell questions the officially accepted line that there are quantifiable externalities that would lead to public good benefits of higher education. He also questions whether higher education really does make for a more productive economy, or whether its use is as an elaborate screening device, subsidised by government. 'If this is investment', he says, 'put your money under the mattress'.

Professor Niall Ferguson worries that universities have become places of 'light learning', in part as a result of their dependence on state funding. 'More' has definitely meant 'worse'. But he too is optimistic that change can occur for the better, that 'new and more sprightly institutions' are emerging to challenge the lumbering established universities. Indeed, if the traditional universities are able to wake up to the possibilities of information and communications technology, then there is no reason why they too cannot be part of a glowing future of 'dreaming spires and speeding modems'.

Finally, chapters ten to twelve showcase three original thinkers from the University of Buckingham. The historian John Clarke offers a comprehensive exploration of the history of Buckingham in the context of two models of a university. He makes a candid assessment and appraisal of whether or not it can be said that the university has succeeded during its twenty-five years. Norman Barry follows with a philosophical examination of the case for privatising higher education in a free society – in the sense of releasing universities from their dependence on state funding and its concomitant regulation. Buckingham's new Vice Chancellor, Terrence Kealey, presents a sparkling account of the private origins of higher education, and the corrupting influence of state funding. He argues that Buckingham bears witness to the viability of a vision of an independent university, that it shows how traditional standards can be maintained without government funding. He looks forward to a rosy future for the university created by 'bold visionaries', one of whom was, Harry S. Ferns, whose paper concludes this volume.

Buckingham at 25

1 HOW NECESSARY ARE UNIVERSITIES?[1]

Alan Peacock

> When a man has learnt his lesson very well, it surely can be
> of little importance where or from whom he learnt it.
>
> Adam Smith

Introduction

In 1774, two years before the appearance of *The Wealth of Nations*,
Adam Smith was consulted by his physician friend William Cullen
about the question of examination for medical degrees. The
College of Physicians of Edinburgh, a very eminent body then as
now, had before it a proposal that medical degrees should be
granted by the Scottish universities only after personal examination of candidates, who would have to produce a certificate prov-
ing that they had studied medicine for at least two years. The
successful candidates would then automatically be granted a licence by the College to practise as doctors. Adam Smith objected
in the strongest terms, arguing that a university education was no
guarantee that graduates would be fit to practise and that such a
proposal would discriminate against private teachers of medicine,
of which in his day there were several of eminence and distinction,

---

1 Revised version of a lecture delivered at the University of Buckingham 25th Anniversary Lecture Series, 13 February 2001.

such as William Hunter. Hence his piquant observation above.[2]

Two hundred years later the same issue was raised about the status of the University College of Buckingham (UCB) Licence, given that the UCB was not then recognised as a university institution as it did not possess a Charter or similar document approved by the Privy Council. Consequently, UCB faced the prospect of discrimination against its graduates, despite the fact that it was widely admitted that they received an education and training at least comparable to that in universities of good standing. The matter was resolved by the application of UCB to become a university, which was eventually successful, despite considerable opposition from influential educationists and the educational press.[3]

However, Adam Smith might have regarded the policy of 'if you can't beat 'em, join 'em' as conceding too much to the conventions of our time. For evidence for his argument, one can cite that very remarkable attack on the cartelisation of universities by Sir Douglas Hague[4], who regards it as anathema to the maintenance of standards of education and research. Hague's work is a landmark in the discussion of the future organisation of training and advancement of knowledge, and foreshadows changes in both the supply of and demand for learning which universities and similar institutions ignore at their peril.

In contrast, the excellent report by the well-known economist

2   Mossner, E. C. & Ross, I. S. (eds) (1977), *The Correspondence of Adam Smith*, Clarendon Press, Oxford, pp 173–9.

3   Peacock, Sir Alan (1986), 'Buckingham's Fight for Independence', *Economic Affairs*, February/March.

4   Hague, Sir Douglas (1991), *Beyond Universities: A New Republic of the Intellect*, Hobart Paper 115, Institute of Economic Affairs.

David Greenaway[5], formerly Professor of Economics at Buckingham, offers a comprehensive appraisal of the financial implications facing governments committed to an expansion in the proportion of school leavers attending higher education institutions on the assumption that the conventional structure of universities remains. An equilibrium between demand for and supply of places, given expansion, has to assume that the funding problems are solved. The report sensibly concludes that the funding problems would entail the wider use of income-contingent loans and tuition fees.

An extension of this scenario would be bound to take into account the influence of technical change not only on the demand for particular types of education but also on the techniques of supplying education itself. Additionally, the opportunity costs of higher education to potential students may be radically affected not only by changes in methods of paying for it but also by the immediate job opportunities which the spread of information technology provides for school leavers. Employers may change their perceptions of a first degree unsullied by practical experience as the 'filter' which guarantees the prospect of recruiting the right sort of staff.

A natural consequence of this debate is to consider whether universities can continue to be the template for the extension and transmission of knowledge. What follows are some speculations on this question with the future of Buckingham in mind, but relevant to the consideration of the future of other British universities too.

5   Greenaway, D. & Haynes, M. (2000), *Funding Universities to Meet National and International Challenges*, School of Economics Policy Report, University of Nottingham.

The argument presented

Universities of the conventional kind expect to enrol students for courses and research who normally are in residence. Imagine a situation where no such institutions existed. Obviously, as a minimum, there would have to be recognised centres of learning able to offer courses leading to degrees which could only be granted to those providing evidence of good standards of performance. Such courses would have to be available in packages which offer explicit guidance to students about how to meet these standards, requiring not only texts but also ways of developing skills and attitudes to learning appropriate to each discipline. In many disciplines this would mean not only the development of reasoning powers, and thus the ability to gauge the strength and weaknesses of arguments, but also, where appropriate, skill in analysing the data on which such arguments are based and in the conduct of experiments. The cards seemed stacked against any aspirant physically separated from the source of the necessary knowledge and who might have to work in conditions which hardly aid the process of understanding.

Technology can transform the position of the isolated student in a whole variety of ways which were virtually unknown when the obvious model, the Open University, was first conceived. The CD-ROM can be used to present on a computer the text of modules for each subject, and also to provide a whole host of back-up material. Prince William need not go to St Andrews, my alma mater, to be presented with the slides of famous historical artefacts, but can stroll through the famous galleries of the world in the company of an expert, and even select and examine those artefacts of particular concern – all on CD. The budding economist and statistician can be given analytical puzzles to solve with full explanation of solutions. In principle, virtual-reality CDs can be created which enable students to fight famous campaigns over again, and even to invent hypothetical alternative strategies for famous battle leaders and their possible results which throw light on the actual decisions taken. Language students can engage in conversations in set pieces of varying degrees of linguistic difficulty and not simply listen to the conversations of others. Music students can have their composition efforts immediately played and even orchestrated, and drama and English students can assign themselves a part in a play. Almost twenty years ago the prominent physicist Professor George Cole, a strong supporter of UCB, claimed that his subject could be taught at Buckingham without the need for laboratories. Experiments could be simulated on computer and new techniques devised which would make it possible for the individual in isolation to do precisely that. On top of this – and only a few examples have been given – students can have access to continuous updating of texts and ancillary information of all kinds through the use of the Web. Nor need the student be completely isolated from those supplying him with these services. Video links can be set up and analysis of progress made through feedback systems.

Of course, universities not only convey knowledge but add to it through research. It seems inconceivable that this function can be successfully carried out by individuals sitting at the end of a computer link or by other institutions. Much depends on whether that research requires a collective effort. As we know, a good deal of individual research, particularly in the humanities field, does not in fact require attendance at the university offering the qualification, and supervision is often infrequent and spasmodic. The crucial requirement is source material from first-class libraries and public record offices. In the case of collective research in medicine, science and engineering, much of this is now carried out in independent institutes or in business establishments. Detailed study of progress in science has destroyed the myth that the universities are the predominant source of new ideas, leaving to industry the task of applied research. (For evidence, consult the symposium edited by Terence Kealey, newly appointed Vice-Chancellor of the University of Buckingham, in *Economic Affairs*, September 2000.[6])

I cannot resist the temptation of recalling that 150 years ago Cardinal Newman, in the Preface to his famous *Idea of a University*, visualised a clear separation between the universities as teaching establishments and research as the function of 'academies' of learned societies physically separated from them: '… to discover and to teach are two distinct functions, and are not commonly united in the same person … The greatest thinkers have been too intent on their subject to admit of interruption; they have been men of absent minds and idiosyncratic habits … The great discoveries in chemistry and electricity were not made in universities … while teaching involves external engagements, the natural home of experiment and speculation is retirement'.[7]

Questions raised by the argument

The first matter raised by this thesis is: is it not simply producing an *ex post* justification for the Open University? The answer is that there are certainly features which correspond to the way the OU operates and I need not catalogue the virtues of that pioneer insti-

---

6   Kealey, T. (*et al.*) (2000), 'Science Policy', in *Economic Affairs*, Journal of the Institute of Economic Affairs, 20.3.

7   Newman, Cardinal John Henry (1852, 1959), *The Idea of a University*, Image Books edition, Garden City, New York, pp 10–11.

tution. However, the system would not make much sense unless students had a choice of institution which fitted their particular requirements and interests. That there is evidence of a demand for university-level education at arm's length, as it were, is instanced in the very considerable number of universities now offering a Distance Learning (DL) approach, but as an alternative method of preparation for a degree which may be taken also by full- or part-time attendance. Indeed, the University of London itself ran DL courses of this kind for the BCom. as far back as the 1930s.

The second matter is how are students to be selected for entry to this approach to knowledge? It is conceivable that the conventional approach of setting entrance standards would be more difficult to operate and therefore more expensive in the case of such aspirants compared with those who have a clear track record confirmed by secondary schools and their equivalents. Here I would offer the bold suggestion that self-selection is the answer. Of course, if entry were to depend solely on the decision of the student, clear signals must be given to students about what the courses and examination entail, and some hurdle erected somewhere along the progression towards a degree which has to be cleared before the students can complete. In any case the DL system can provide continuous evidence of progress.

The third matter raises the very complicated question of finance. One important reason given for insisting on entrance qualifications is to try to control the failure rate in universities, it being conventionally argued that the rate of failure also gauges the extent to which taxpayers' money is being 'wasted'. If there were no such control, the government and local authorities would be at risk if numbers registered at universities were simply a function of those willing to enrol. If present rules about student support are applied it would be very difficult to operate a 'free entry' system for university institutions without agreeing with them to finance a given quota of students, including both the grant component and the direct funding which universities at present receive for teaching purposes. If a university exceeded its quota it would have to charge fees which differentiated between students admitted as part of the quota who had reached some qualificatory standard and those who did not who would have to pay their way. This tangle can be unravelled by private universities such as Buckingham who fix their own charges and who otherwise offer educational substitutes for other universities or who follow more closely the new pattern suggested by the general argument. It is then up to students to find means of funding, not necessarily from their own pocket. This is compatible with the educational innovation of a two-year degree without the traditional long vacation, for the degree of financial discrimination is thereby considerably reduced.

That funding for higher education should be tied so closely to conventional methods of access can in any case lead to all manner of injustices, particularly those associated with the requirement of taking a degree within some rigid determined time limit and normally on leaving school. (Greenaway and Haynes report that 80 per cent of university new entrants are below the age of 24.3.) Even if state or local government finance is made available for other classes of students, the same degree of automaticity of funding rarely operates. This problem can only be solved by being clear about the principles of entitlement to be applied to the financing of higher education. I for one would like to see every individual credited with an educational 'competence', to use an old-fashioned term, which he or she could use for any recognised form of tertiary education and which would be available at, say, eighteen years of age but which need not necessarily be used all at once and within a very restricted time period. Economists and social scientists will recognise this proposal as akin to those which have been put forward for the reform of the welfare state by which individuals are credited with savings accounts to enable them to finance pensions, access to health services and housing, and I see no reason why an educational component should not be added. Of course, such an idea would require a costing exercise which might reveal some rather terrifying results if the 'competence' were based on the real cost per student in universities. A conflict between equity and efficiency would almost certainly emerge.

I come now to the fourth and most important question: how can the full benefits of higher education be transmitted without the close personal links between students and staff? At one time, the counter-argument would emphasise the importance of pastoral care with the university or college laying down standards of behaviour and exercising disciplinary procedures if these standards were breached – remember Dr Spooner rusticating a student at Oxford and demanding that he proceed to leave Oxford immediately by the town drain! Now all that seems to be left is the offence of cheating in examinations, though even this has sometimes been condoned. This residual offence draws attention to the one crucial moral judgement on which there is a consensus in universities and which should be accepted by all their members – the integrity of their scholarship and research and therefore transparency of argument and open access to the testing procedures on which they are based. In short, scientific enquiry must rest on a moral foundation. It is difficult to imagine that this can be satisfactorily conveyed by any form of communication, even video link, other than close and continuing contact between scholars of differing ability and experience. But in case this sounds rather dull and forbidding, one must add that such personal contact has not only the function of setting an example, but also the opportunity to enthuse the student and hopefully to instil the idea of the intense satisfaction to be gained from acquiring understanding and knowledge for their own sake – although the inspirational gift is not one with which academics are universally endowed.

Even if we assume that the process of learning and understanding is substantially promoted by the community benefits of academe we have to ask ourselves whether physical presence of the students in a single university location is a *sine qua non* in the list of requirements to complete a satisfactory course of study. Of course, for some students, frequently those who are ill focused in their ideas about what they wish to study and why and how to study at all, it is so. There will be those who value direct and continuous contact with both teachers and fellow-students but for whom it is essential only to have the opportunity available on a part-time basis or as a fall-back if they are in difficulty. But there are also those for whom the opportunity cost of being part of an academic community of a traditional character is too high. Changes in social patterns reflected in one-parent families and perceived responsibilities to aged or disabled relatives, even being part of the prison population or required to perform community service, are examples that come to mind. Rapid changes in economic opportunities and the associated risks in obtaining employment may alter preference patterns of young people who choose to enter the labour market on leaving school but who may graft on study at university level either in parallel with their work opportunities or in series by becoming mature full-time or part-time students in later life. Such students may indeed forgo the benefits of the traditional university system, but in learning about life the hard way they can acquire motivation, experience and understanding by other means.

Some radical conclusions

The first conclusion is that the essential functions of a higher education remain as they ever were. We expect students to emerge from the system as persons who have learnt not only how to process information and produce innovative ideas but who are also imbued with tolerance and understanding and intellectual honesty. However, the process is a voluntary one, and in the end students will exercise sovereignty in deciding where, when and how to study. They will certainly need help and will demand advice in making choices, but advisers are needed who can provide collateral information of an unbiased kind. Apart from the value judgement in this statement, I postulate that the changes in our society that I have already outlined will accelerate this desire for freedom of action in seeking the benefits of higher education and will extend to the demand for that supplied by schools.

The second conclusion is that potential students will more and more demand facilities for study which fit with their own perceptions of a career and the place of education in its time profile. They may conclude that this requires them to follow the conventional path to university, but viewed against the alternatives open to them. In other words, the universities' monopoly of modes of delivery of the elements of higher education already identified is likely to be eroded. This is not only because of the demand for flexibility by the customer, the student, but because new modes of delivery based on modern technology can be more efficient in the sense that similar benefits accrue to the student and usually at a lower cost to them or their sponsors. It is also claimed that the provision of DL courses galvanises academics into being much more responsive to individual student demands.

Universities have responded to the threat of competition partly by absorption of satellite colleges and institutions which exchange their full autonomy for the right to award degrees, and partly by developing ancillary services which may help them to rebut charges of exclusivity or remoteness and which conveniently help their budgetary position. Such are self-financing research parks, and MBA and other vocational courses. It is fascinating to be on the sidelines of this activity, observing the tug-of-war between entrenched university bureaucracies trying to impose inappropriate rules on innovatory developments of this kind and directors of such institutions who have to bear the risks of being self-financing and who demand the necessary freedom of action to be able to survive in what can be highly competitive markets. (An amusing example concerns the attempt by a certain university to retire a highly respected tea lady working in its most successful independent institute. The protest by the head of this institute was met by typical bureaucratic inflexibility until he pointed out that he had one group of appointments under his control and he would therefore appoint her a consultant. Exposure to ridicule can be a powerful weapon!)

The third conclusion is that other methods of access to higher education of university standard are not simply to be regarded as second-best arrangements tacked on to existing university institutions. The traditional method of imparting information, acquiring knowledge and appreciating its significance does not necessarily represent the pinnacle of pedagogic achievement but is one of several alternatives, albeit an important one, which differ in their comparative advantage, as viewed by those who demand their services. Furthermore, as has been repeatedly stressed, if the value of education is in the eye of the beholder, then he or she has to consider the opportunity cost of going through the process. A corollary of this argument is that these alternative methods should be considered on their own merits, and barriers to entry removed. Those of us with long memories recall how the forces of reaction within university circles endeavoured to prevent the award of university status to Buckingham. Now more subtle means of discrimination against interlopers are being practised. It is bad for a university's image not to pay at least lip-service to the application of new technologies to the learning process. However, interlopers can be kept in their place by supporting publication of 'performance indicators' which are biased towards traditional university activities.

An example of an adventurous alternative to the conventional pattern is provided by the proposed University of the Highlands and Islands, which is having to clear a succession of hurdles in order to obtain official recognition despite the thought behind its planning and the commitment of distinguished academics – Sir Graham Hills and Professor Alistair MacFarlane, both former Vice-Chancellors, no less – which are far more extensive than those demanded in the setting up of the 'new' universities such as York and Sussex.[8] The dispersion of population in the Highlands and Islands, and fears of further depopulation (not so far confirmed, as it happens), have prevented successive governments,

---

8   Hills, Sir Graham (1997), 'The University of the Highlands & Islands: Scotland's first Regional University', in *A Future for Scottish Higher Education*, COSHEP (Committee of Scottish Higher Education Principals), pp. 86–96.

hidebound by the conception of a university as a place of fixed lo-cation, from meeting the repeated request to establish a university in Inverness. There are, however, a number of widely scattered in-stitutes and colleges in the Highlands and Islands which conduct research and higher education learning. The general idea is that these institutes should become the local centres to which students can gravitate instead of having to leave families and homes, serv-ing the dual purpose of reducing the considerable expense of going to large centres of learning a long distance away and of combining easy access to teaching media with opportunities for continuing contact with local staff and fellow students. Obviously such an idea assumes that modern technology is a precondition for im-proving educational methods as well as a more economical way of making them effective. Indeed, that is claimed by Professors Hills and MacFarlane as more than an assumption – they argue strongly that the learning routine built round the traditional series of lec-tures is a poor method of communicating information, segment-ing knowledge into watertight compartments just at a time when the boundaries are being rapidly changed. All knowledge must be based on a common core of skills which ensure that students are reasonably numerate and articulate and above all find it in them-selves to wish to acquire them. This emphasises once again my principal argument that the higher education system has to accept that it is likely to become more and more demand led, fitting with a different rhythm and pattern into the career life-cycle as per-ceived by those who seek to improve themselves, with perceptions changing through time.

Whither Buckingham?

My contentions fully justify the setting up of Buckingham as an independent private university. Thirty-five years ago I considered that the founding fathers exaggerated the extent to which a monolithic university system would stifle freedom of thought. The mastermind behind the massive 1960s expansion, Lionel Robbins, was deeply conscious of the possible effects of state funding on academic freedom; and one need only read the clauses which he drafted in the Charter of the University of York to observe how anxious he was to prevent dismissal of staff because they held unpopular political views. Moreover, he expressed his full approval of the Buckingham experiment by his attendance at the presentation of its Charter in 1983. However, today I am inclined to think that the founding fathers were more prescient than I was, for the pressures on our state universities to follow the dictates of political correctness have increased. The only rider I would attach to this statement is that these pressures extend throughout society, and Buckingham cannot be entirely immune from them.

One great virtue of being a private university lies in the internalisation of bureaucratic control and the concomitant potential to be able to respond quickly to a rapidly changing market situation. Buckingham places particular emphasis on the two-year degree system and the recognition that the probability of success in surviving its rigours is not to be measured in terms of rigid entry requirements. The manifestation of their success lies in the silencing of criticism that they are only means for increasing demand for places and result in poor degree performances – I know of senior academic figures who are deeply envious of this degree of flexibility. My analysis suggests that Buckingham, too, must be ever watchful of the changing preferences of potential students who, in an international market, may have a greater degree of choice. In this regard, the two-year degree involving full attendance may have to become one of several alternatives on offer. Buckingham could be better placed than state universities in gauging the degree of change necessary and in the speed of implementation, but one can never tell when the dam may break and the university cartel may begin to fall apart at the seams. Buckingham should never seek the dissolution of its distinguished Academic Advisory Council (AAC), which offers the guarantee that the external examining system is firmly in place. While modular systems lay much more emphasis on continuous assessment, which makes external examining difficult, Buckingham might indeed experiment with how such a system can be sensibly monitored from outside. The AAC is a unique feature in university governance and should be given much more prominence in its public relations literature.

Nothing in what has been said is meant to convey the idea that there is a unique virtue in universities being simply suppliers of ideas and data issued through computer networks. All that is being argued is that continuous residence combined with traditional methods of teaching in small groups, and benefiting from dedicated research near by, is not necessarily the ideal to which every academic institution need aspire. That said, there is no reason why Buckingham should not continue to centre its organisation in a well-established and effective tradition which suits a particular student and research clientèle. Indeed, while apparently every effort is being made by government to frustrate state universities in attempts to recreate the underlying conditions which retain the efficacy of sensible, traditional methods, notably in the crude attempts to measure their efficiency, Buckingham should be advantageously situated, being free from the imposition of uniformity which state financing of universities requires. There is, I suppose, a natural propensity to measure its performance against that of others and to de-emphasise the differences with other institutions, if only to maintain friendly relations. However, to allow itself to accept the criteria of performance laid down by governments and their academic advisers, and also the weight given to each of these criteria, would be a betrayal of its ethos.

2 WHO OWNS THE UNIVERSITIES? – THE BATTLE FOR UNIVERSITY INDEPENDENCE; THE BATTLE AGAINST THE DEPENDENCY CULTURE
Graham Hills

The nature of the battle

This chapter is about the freedom of British universities. It is about their transformation from an abject state of financial dependence on central government, in which their will has been sapped, to a situation where they can be at the forefront of changes made possible by the Internet revolution. It is about their possible disestablishment in the face of opposition from students, staff, vice-chancellors and industry, all lulled into resignation by power-hungry government.

The case for a more sensible basis of funding is argued as the key to affordable higher education and to the creation of a regulated market of university opportunities. Unless the cost and benefits of both teaching and research are clearly understood, then muddle will persist, and with it the debilitating effects of under-funding, under-investment and continued decline.

The intellectual independence of the universities is inseparable from their financial independence. Both in a managerial sense and in that of civilised values, British universities have increasingly come under the sway of big government. It has used its financial muscle to coerce compliance from the universities in matters large and small. The level of bureaucracy is everywhere insupportable. The effort of individual universities to improve their positions in the myriad of league tables of measurable performance is as futile as the zero-sum philosophy on which all such discrimination is based.

The slide into penury began in the second half of the 20th century. There was no shortage of warnings from perceptive individuals of the dangers of 'he who pays the piper'. But collectively the universities became doomed as they concentrated their efforts on defending their privileges, which turned out to be no more than long holidays and low salaries. The occasional concerted effort to fend off government always faltered because the collegiate will turned out to be a myth. Attempts to threaten government were dismissed as the bluff they always were. Eventually, the universities' preoccupation with their dwindling finances became their sole concern.

The abiding question of who was doing what for whom and at what price was scorned by the dons as vulgar managerialism. Adam Smith's required relationship between buyer and seller, spelt out by him with particular regard to professors and their student customers, was ignored. As the economics of higher education became increasingly muddied, out of the blue stepped New Labour, to decree a token fee for all undergraduates. The question of student fees became another political football, bringing the curious spectacle of the Liberals and Conservatives arguing together for their abolition!

The clear and only solution to these problems was to put the business of the universities onto businesslike foundations. Such a simple solution was disregarded by the ancient universities as a threat to their cosy existence. In their customary Byzantine way, they would lead the resistance to all reform, simply by not saying 'yes' to anything. They knew they could count on their allies, not least the vice-chancellors.

So, in the end, the universities failed to summon up the will to do anything but sit on their hands. Time and again they, and particularly their vice-chancellors, earned their sobriquet of a hot bed of cold feet as, little by little, their status ebbed away.

Other vital issues, mostly stemming from the ICT revolution, hardly intruded, and when they did they were set aside. The same fate awaited the earnest recommendations of, first, the Dearing Inquiry[1] of 1997, and then those even more far-reaching which emanated from the Bologna Declaration – where 29 European countries pledged to reform the structures of their higher education in 'a convergent way', to create the 'European Space for Higher Education'.[2] Ron, now Lord, Dearing concluded that there was much to be gained from a lower-level, broadly based first degree on which subsequent more specialised and professional studies could be built. This was not only the affordable basis of mass higher education but pedagogically a sounder basis for the lifelong learning ethos being advocated by governments worldwide.

Within five years this issue had reached international attention, but from another point of view – namely the desirability of some commonality of degree programmes which would then allow students worldwide to intercalate their studies in other universities and other countries, the much-respected Erasmus principle. The idea of a common ladder of attainment, first mooted in the Sorbonne Declaration of May 1998, signed by a limited num-

---

1   National Committee of Inquiry into Higher Education (1997), *Higher Education in the Learning Society* (the 'Dearing Report'), HMSO, London.

2   For further details see http://www.crue.upm.es/eurec/bolognaexplanation. htm.

ber of European countries, was too attractive to be dismissed out of hand. Indeed, against all the odds the process of harmonisation was signed into being by a large number of universities. In 2001, the Salamanca meeting of the Convention of European Higher Education endorsed the 'three-plus-two-plus-three' model for all students.[3]

And where was Britain? Nowhere to be seen. The matter had been discussed by universities in the UK and then shelved.

The fact is that British universities have now stumbled a long way down a path designed for a small élite whose research interests could once be comfortably afforded from their endowments and specific research grants. By failing miserably to think intelligently about the nature and cost of mass higher education, the universities have collectively stifled the vitality and confidence of all but a few of their number. Moreover, by imbuing generations of students with their own culture of dependency, they have made a major contribution to the dependency culture of Britain as a whole.

The once independent universities, free to operate as the global institutions they have always been, have given way to timorous, fractious bodies concerned only to balance the books.

Putting Humpty Dumpty together again may be difficult, but there remains a core of stubborn academics who believe it still worth while to try. The tree of liberty could still be refreshed.

The passive state of British universities

A mere 40 years ago, British universities were largely independent

---

3   http://147.83.2.29/salamanca2001/documents/main_texts/bologna.htm.

organisations. They owned their assets and derived their income from student grants, often paid by local authorities. Such uniformity of practice as existed stemmed largely from the fact that so many redbrick universities had been colleges of other, larger universities, most particularly London University. Although there were wide variations in course arrangements and curricula, there were agreed standards of qualifications, mostly self-regulated by the gentle oversight of external examiners. At the end of the day, the Privy Council and a benign University Grants Committee kept a watchful but distant eye on things. A specific Treasury minute precluded any further interference, most of all by the Department of Education. There was also a wide range of local boards to oversee school examinations. They helped to harmonise the learning requirements of universities with those of the schools.

This happy scene did not last. Larger numbers of students, especially ex-servicemen, made larger demands on resources. The Robbins Report[4] recommended an heroic expansion of higher education to admit, in principle at least, every adult able to benefit from it. Foolishly, this was interpreted as an excuse to expand linearly the existing arrangements with their costly emphasis on specialised honours degrees as the norm.

The influence of Oxbridge was critical. Normally happy in their seclusion, Oxbridge worthies were wheeled out to sit on every foundation committee of the new universities. They knew or cared only about Newman's ideals, and a dozen or so Oxbridge shadows formed the greater part of the Robbins brigade. The Robbins' principle itself was quickly forgotten.

---

4   Committee on Higher Education (1963), *Higher Education: Report* (the 'Robbins Report'), HMSO, Cmnd 2154, London.

There was certainly a considerable reservoir of talent available to fill the extra places. Although conservatives complained that 'more means worse', the battle to widen access was gradually won. Christopher Ball put the lid on one set of doubters in his timely reference to 'more means different'.[5] The sad and abiding result, however, was that both references were wrong. More did not mean worse but more did not mean different. The aim of higher education remained that of imparting explicit knowledge to the neglect or exclusion of other kinds of knowledge, particularly skills. When, 25 years later, the university system again doubled in size, this time to accommodate the then polytechnics, they too would be burdened with the expense of higher education to the honours level, to be provided by research-based departments dedicated to research-based knowledge. Again, Oxbridge had prevailed.

The new competition on a now steeply sloping playing field had another disastrous consequence. New rules, epitomised by the Research Assessment Exercise (RAE), led to a progressive narrowing of the options. An already monolithic system of higher education became even more so. Diversity, which is the normal vehicle for evolutionary change, was squeezed out, and with it the opportunity for gradual as opposed to revolutionary reform.

Constitutional stalemate

The possibility of an orderly, flexible response to the government's determination to bully the universities into submission was progressively reduced by two factors. Postwar Britain was smitten

---

5   Chancellor of Derby University and Chairman of the Global University Alliance. He founded the national Campaign for Learning.

with industrial decline, as evidenced by its still-low productivity and inept technology transfer. The universities were open to the criticism that for all the money spent on them there was precious little to show for it. Throughout the 1980s and 1990s successive initiatives were dreamt up to commercialise the scientific brainpower of Britain. The universities did themselves no favours by their offhand response to this kind of government plea.

To this cultural defect was added another hurdle, that of the ineptitude of the body supposed to speak up for the universities as a whole. It is difficult to describe a collection of vice-chancellors. They are appointed as prima donnas and they behave like prima donnas, even *en masse*. As a result, the then collective body, the Committee of Vice-Chancellors and Principals (CVCP), now recently rebranded as Universities UK, was and is unable to make the smallest decision. It is like a senate writ large, a debating society more interested in form than in outcomes.

Given these factors, it is understandable that governments of the left and of the right grew increasingly frustrated Every year, the cry went up from the vice-chancellors that not one more student could be accommodated, but every year the numbers swelled. Twenty years on, the unit cost of undergraduate higher education had halved, by default.

The obvious results of progressively tighter funding were crowded auditoria, obsolete apparatus, narrowing options, departmental closures and even campus shutdowns. The less obvious but more insidious results were to be felt on staff morale, especially as it conditioned the quality of academic appointments to carry out that most important of tasks, the inspiration of the young.

The unions should also take some of the blame. Central bargaining with central government over centrally determined salary scales was another symptom of the 1960s illnesses. As in the case of schoolteachers, the unions were concerned only with money, leaving the priceless quality of professional competence for others to worry about. The only political demonstrations were in support of salaries and ironically against the fees that might have augmented those salaries.

The decades over which the universities lost their confidence and their influence were the fruit of that cast of mind best described by the word pusillanimous. Perhaps the rate of change in the world at large was too much. Perhaps the overthrow of the academic ethos of explicit certain knowledge by the softer, more flexible ways of modernity damaged their *raison d'être*. Notably, the mathematicians resisted the computer age. Whatever the cause, the universities lost their nerve and their freedom.

New dawnings

But not everybody joined the throng of mourners. There were those, like Professor Ferns,[6] who saw all this coming, who believed that the National Audit Office would not duck its statutory duty to examine the finances of universities, now largely dependent on government funding. These voices said, 'Wake up. If universities are to retain their historic role of independence of thought and action, they had better find the financial basis of doing so.'

If there was no reason why universities should be paid for by governments, there was every reason why they should not. All those industries that had escaped the well-meaning but disastrous noose of nationalisation had emerged into the sunlight to trade on

---

6　See the final chapter in this volume.

their own terms, to invest in their futures and to pay the salaries required to attract the very best people.

To many academics, however, the idea of universities being businesses or even businesslike is distasteful. To them, universities are above the sordid affairs of merchants, of profit, loss and savings. There are some universities which can afford to take that view. They are small in number and they seldom do. To others the parable of the talents requires them to use their best endeavours to put their resources to good use. That does not imply that universities should be a party to sharp practice but, as the Quakers and others amply demonstrated, it is possible to be both fair and profitable. That is surely the line to be taken by the universities.

However, there is a more profound reason for insisting that universities take a businesslike view of their business. Before the first signs in 2001 of demand saturation, there had been a lengthening queue of applicants keen to enter university. The message from government, from families and from schools was 'get qualified'. There were to be good jobs for graduates, and possibly none for the rest. While it could be argued that not all the actual entrants had the stamina to stay the honours course, the question of student quality had not emerged in any significant way.

The reason for Britain's low age participation rate throughout the decades from the 1960s to the 1990s was simple. Access was limited by resources. The perennial injustice of those times was not that the right to entry was limited by arbitrary academic achievement but that the money available was insufficient to meet the cost of enrolling all those who were formally qualified. This failure to invest in people became the basis of the argument for more prudent use of educational resources and for a better basis of funding, not to satisfy marginal improvements in living standards of those already in the lifeboat but to meet the basic costs of those who were still trying to clamber aboard.

To those who rejected the complacent acceptance of the status quo, that is, the present system of deficiency funding from central government, this was a moral issue. For every well-heeled middle-class undergraduate enjoying free higher education, there was another potential undergraduate from a lower social class having to go without. To those students opposing fees who marched to the cry 'Abolish Fees – Education is a Right', it needed to be said that this right was a myth as long as access was arbitrarily restricted.

It was, therefore, on the moral grounds of maximising access, of using resources to maximum advantage and of having some regard for equity that newer and fairer procedures of funding universities were advocated. One of these, involving subsidised tuition fees for all students, was identified early on as the most equitable way of increasing student numbers, as well as the income of universities, by allowing them to charge fully economic fees to all their customers. The very act of bringing transparent values to bear would also bring a note of reality to all those involved, including government, industry, parents and, of course, the students themselves.

Affordable universities; fair fees for all

The single, simple financial reform advocated in this paper is in two parts:

First, the bad news is that universities will need to determine the economic, market costs of what they do, that is, teaching undergraduates, promoting research and rendering other services, and *charge their customers accordingly*.

These costs will vary widely from subject to subject and from university to university. This is no one-price-one-fit area of human activity. These costs can nevertheless be met by charging the students who will exercise their judgement as to value for money. There is every evidence that quality always wins. Wise people buy not the cheapest but the best they can afford.

The good news, however, is that it is not the tradition in Britain to pay low taxes in order to be able to afford expensive private education. No scheme of university funding making such demands in Britain would have a chance of succeeding, justified though they may be. It is here, then, that government, central or local, steps in to offer each student registered at the university of their choice a scholarship *to meet the greater part of the basic cost of their course*. The key word here is 'basic', and it would be for government and universities to negotiate these basic costs. This would not be a difficult or a definitive exercise. The numbers might need to be constantly adjusted in the light of experience but, for the purpose of this argument, the costs can be thought of as rounded averages sufficient to meet the basic costs of each subject area.

If, then, the transition from deficiency funding to fee-based, market income is to be financially neutral to *both* students and government, it is essential that the basic cost be kept low. It is proposed here that it be the agreed average cost of a three-year foundation degree on the Bologna model.

All universities, such as the Liberal Arts Universities of the United States, offering essentially foundation degrees, could afford to run profitably on this basis. Since it is argued, on academic grounds, that all students would benefit by taking such a foundation degree, then no student would be excluded on financial grounds from any university. The basic fees they would be asked to pay could even be fully funded for three years. For the great majority of undergraduate students their new status as fee-paying, albeit subsidised, customers would empower them to expect and require the highest level of education that their fee would pay for. This alone would justify this reform. It would place an immediate premium on more effective, more attractive and better-quality tuition, for which at present there is no incentive whatsoever.

For the minority of students wishing to go farther, for example, to the professional, Masters level of medical doctor, accountant, architect, engineer or lawyer, this would require further periods of full-time or part-time study to be paid for, not by the state, but by loans, employers and from job experience. If the notion of the Bologna degree is developed in terms of what is called the 'New Learning Paradigm', then there would be ample opportunities for such senior students to earn their way as tutors or instructors of junior students attending foundation courses. Again the circle is squared to advantage.

What is meant by the New Learning Paradigm? Briefly it is the replacement of chalk-and-talk by the studied use of machine knowledge, for example, the Internet, and problem-based learning on the basis of case studies. These two new learning tools are remarkable in two ways: firstly, in their effectiveness as vehicles for the transfer of explicit knowledge on the one hand and implicit, tacit knowledge on the other; and secondly, in the fact that they cost so little. Indeed, MIT has just made the extraordinary gesture of putting all its course materials onto the Internet, where they are available free of charge.

That expensive instrument of undergraduate instruction, namely the research professor, will now need to be used more circumspectly. Given that research should not and need not be subsidised, as it is now, out of the costs of teaching, then it follows that the basic fees of the foundation degree courses can be kept low and affordable.

For research students, the future is surely clear. Their sponsors should regard them as the valuable research assistants they really are. There is no excuse not to pay them the rate for the job. And they would still be the cheapest form of labour. Again it is necessary to harp on the question of who is paying whom for what. Research can also be businesslike, and suddenly the problems of dual funding fall away.

The Department for Education and Employment (DfEE) might demur at losing a bit of its empire. But it is and always was a virtual empire, the fifth wheel on the coach. It knows little about the nuts and bolts of education and is best kept out of the picture.

This simple device of rerouting the existing government subsidy of higher education through the student body rather than through the universities themselves has much merit. First, it satisfies the golden rule of economics – *Never Subsidise the Supplier*. By subsidising instead the student customer, the new procedure invites every university to add value to what it does. Some students will want to pay more for more, be it college residence, foreign experience or technological skills. But as long as the basic cost is met for all students, then equity is satisfied.

The new scheme is also an incentive for universities to reexplore their market niches, to find new ways of satisfying and creating demand, and to use new ways of investing in their assets.

Almost at a stroke, the dispiriting environment of the supplicant is transformed into the beckoning horizons of the independent optimist.

So will it work?

The shoot-out

The alternative way of funding universities described here has the advantage over all others of realising a bottom-up transaction between the main beneficiary, the individual undergraduate, and the supplier, in this case the individual university. It is this face-to-face engagement in which values, benefits and obligations become transparent and reduce the lumbering of remote bodies to the human dimension of the direct choice and reward of the individual student.

The subsidy as a scholarship might be thought to be a euphemism for voucher, a word not lightly used here. It is currently a dirty word with unacceptable political overtones. The success of voucher systems in North America has also been derided there as creeping socialism, although the supplementary benefits were available to both private and public schools. Under the last Conservative administration, a simple variant, the Assisted Places Scheme, was condemned by Old and New Labour as élitist, selective, divisive and unfair. So this is tiger country in which we must tread carefully.

If, on the other hand, as a scholarship, bursary or voucher-in-disguise, it is universally available to every British citizen who chooses to use it, then it is a universal benefit. There is no hidden political agenda. It is still a reward for merit because it is only cashable at the college or university of higher and further education at which the application is accepted. Indeed, everyone is involved on their merit – the student, the college or university and the government, which, if it wants to be re-elected, should not be ungenerous in agreeing the value of the scholarship or voucher.

Another significant virtue of the subsidised fee at the heart of the new funding procedure is its inherent flexibility. All the component parts of the deal are open to adjustment to suit particular circumstances. The aggregated sum of all the subsidies, scholarships and vouchers will need to reflect the values and wealth of the day. A rich country, like the United States, is happy to operate with low levels of subsidy. An emerging country might need to be more generous in support of its students. A fair price for every aspect will need to be evidently so whether it is university salaries, student fees, residential facilities, international exchanges, and so on. There is a need for transparency but no need for government. The customer-contract principle is sacred and will deliver and maintain the necessary efficiencies.

The system described here has therefore many social and political advantages. Combining as it does the best of all values, it is hard to see that it has any defects. As a technical, purely financial exercise, it has been examined by supporters and opponents alike, and because it is flexible it can be made to work in good times and bad times. Who, then, could object to it?

The answer is, I am afraid, almost everybody. We have come full circle from representing the plight of universities as dire, debilitating and acceptable to nobody, but still not so desperate as to stimulate a willingness to risk change. Notwithstanding its attractions, the new funding procedure may still be seen as too big a risk because it seems too large a change. Actually it is little more than an exercise in musical chairs, but every participant in higher education will immediately see the advantages for some as a disadvantage for them.

To the students, the only way seems down. For two generations, the lucky few have enjoyed free higher education at every level and they cannot accommodate even zero fees. They care little about the nature and quality of education for all. For them their degree certificate is everything. Oxbridge undergraduates care a great deal about their privileged existence. It is not threatened by anything but they will jib like the rest at paying anything for it.

The universities themselves, as typified by their vice-chancellors, are those prisoners in the cave who have adjusted to their lot. If they persist in defending the model of supposedly identical universities – although everyone knows that standards vary considerably – all offering the same honours degree, then it is difficult to see how this unaffordable model can survive. Few will have experienced the quality and vitality of Liberal Arts in the United States. Few, if any, will therefore volunteer for this role in the UK.

Although, therefore, a British version of the kaleidoscopic colours of North American higher education might beckon as a place to be, the journey back to get there may be simply asking too much. Irreversibility is a word to be feared under all circumstances, even though it is the defining quality of life.

Nature escapes the deadly hand of irreversibility by mutation and diversity. One new university embracing the New Learning Paradigm and prospering from the new funding procedures would do more for the cause of reform than any amount of argument. It was, and perhaps still is, one of the hopes of the projected University of the Highlands and Islands of Scotland – perhaps also a way forward for the University of Buckingham?

The University of the Highlands and Islands of Scotland[7] is to be the first university since the Middle Ages founded by a local

7   The University of the Highlands and Islands is a new, largely virtual university. Its mission is to establish 'for the Highlands and Islands of Scotland a collegiate university which will reach the highest standards and play a pivotal role in our educational, economic, social and cultural development'. For more details see www.uhi.ac.uk.

community and not captive to any existing universities. Its greatest asset was the clean sheet of paper on which to inscribe its objectives, which were to found a collegiate federation of small colleges rather as in Oxbridge but separated by tens or hundreds of miles. Already the pressure on it to conform is mounting. Even in the new nearly independent Scotland, the message is the same – 'Conform or do without'. And this is the easy route to reform.

The other route, that of requesting established universities to experiment with alternative procedures, is as close as it comes to inviting turkeys to celebrate Christmas. As a one-time vice-chancellor sitting numbly with my fellows in the Senate House of London University, I used to ask myself the question 'How much worse will it have to get for these clever chaps to change?' (They were all chaps.) The answer remains, as ever, 'Quite a lot.'

3 A FINE BALANCING ACT – FREEDOM AND ACCOUNTABILITY
Diana Warwick

Like Janus, universities face both ways. They look to the public purse for the core funding necessary to carry out their primary functions of teaching and research. They look to private sources to enhance and diversify their income through the recruitment of overseas and part-time students, the sponsorship of research and training, and the development of links with business and the community. The income profile of universities reflects this with some £7.5 billion (62 per cent of total income) deriving from public funds and the remainder from private sources.

In this sense universities occupy a *fairly* unique position, straddling as they do both the private and public sectors. They are big businesses in their own right, innovators and entrepreneurs contributing to wealth creation and the knowledge-based economy. They are also, increasingly, instruments for the delivery of public policy agendas and agents of social and economic change. Public funding comes with strings attached – the 'something for something' principle.

The challenge lies in developing systems and structures for accountability and funding that are sensitive to these diverse objectives and functions. It is right that, as big spenders of public funds, universities should be accountable to Parliament and the electorate for the use of those funds. But this responsibility must be balanced against the need for flexible and responsive systems that do not stifle innovation and which allow entrepreneurialism to flourish.

This fine, but crucial, balancing act has not yet been achieved. The current systems still burden universities with unnecessary red tape which is time-consuming, costly and restricting. The time for reform is long overdue.

The nature, scale and cost of the current accountability regime have recently been assessed for the Higher Education Funding Council for England (HEFCE) by PA Consulting. They concluded that the direct and indirect costs of the present system stand at more than £250 million per annum. This is equivalent to 5 per cent of the total HEFCE budget. These are costs that universities can ill afford. Universities have had years of real-terms cuts in per student funding. Only recently has this trend been reversed. Such hard-won funding is needed to finance the core activities of universities. It should not be drained away in bureaucracy.

The main cost areas for accountability are:

- the Quality Assurance Agency (QAA);
- the Research Assessment Exercise (RAE);
- the cost of bidding for the increasing range of special initiative funding; and
- the cost of providing more and more data about students, finances and staff.

These are in addition to the financial accountability regime delivered through financial memoranda between the funding councils and their respective government departments, and between the funding councils and each of their respective institutions. Each in turn is accountable to Parliament through the Public Accounts

Committee. Following the Comprehensive Spending Review in 1998 there is also the development of a new costing system – the Transparency Review – which will facilitate the reporting of spending of both public and private funds. This will be in place in all research-intensive universities this year and all institutions next year.

Accountability for funds from the private sector is governed by universities' contracts – implicit and explicit – with students at all levels of study, with companies and charities for research and services, and as a condition of charitable grants.

Some welcome moves have already been made to reduce the burden of quality assessment in higher education through government proposals for a new 'light touch' arrangement whereby university departments that have achieved good scores in the current round of subject reviews (at least three scores of 3 and three scores of 4 on the six factors assessed) would be exempt from external review in the next round, apart from a small proportion which would be sampled by agreement to provide the necessary benchmarking of good practice. Taken with the planned further reduction in the average length of reviews, the aim is to secure a reduction of 40 per cent or more in the volume of review activity from the existing arrangements. This should lead to savings in the sector both in time and money. But it is a small part of the £250 million accountability bill identified by PA Consulting. More radical reform is needed if this cost is to be brought down so that more money can flow into supporting the core business of universities.

Universities UK's recent review of funding options, led by Sir William Taylor, helps to provide the context for the £250 million. The review had a dual purpose: to identify the funding requirement of the sector and to assess the strengths and weaknesses of the options for meeting that requirement. The review was partly a response to the then Secretary of State for Education and Employment, David Blunkett's, call for a rigorous debate on the future funding of higher education at the time of his speech at the University of Greenwich in February 2000.

With the aid of independent consultants, the final report from the Funding Options Review, *New Directions for Higher Education Funding*, March 2001,[1] identified a minimum additional funding requirement of £900 million per annum by 2004/05 for the higher education sector. This figure needs to be set in the context of the significant damage that has been done by many years of underfunded expansion. The last 20 years have seen a reduction in funding per student of more than 50 per cent. Average staff/student ratios have moved from 1:9 to 1:17 and, if the money for research in that average unit of funding is included, to 1:23.

The recent boost in funding from the government is welcome, but much of it has been needed to catch up on the past underinvestment. More investment is needed if the future is to be secured. The Funding Options Review report identified the following needs within the £900 million requirement:

- To maintain in 2003/04 the purchasing power of current levels of Funding Council grant, taking into account the likelihood of pay increases coming in above assumed inflation levels, would require £75 million in 2004/05.
- The sum of £170 million allocated for recruitment and retention of staff is £100 million adrift from the £275 million

---

1   Universities UK (2001), *New Directions for Higher Education Funding* (the 'Taylor Report'), London.

in the Bett Report, which remains the best-worked source of such calculations available.

- To meet the statutory requirements for institutions to offer equal pay for work of equal value could cost up to £100 million per annum.
- To correct under-investment in infrastructure and fully to meet the requirement of the Disability Discrimination Act could cost some £500 million, against provision in existing plans of £250 million.
- To enhance to 20 per cent, as recommended in the recent Select Committee report,[2] the so-called post-code premium designed to raise recruitment and retention of disadvantaged students would require another £75 million on top of what has already been allocated for this purpose.

The Funding Options Review also analysed the range of options for meeting this funding requirement. At the heart of the debate about possible options are questions about the balance between public and private contributions to higher education, the way in which such contributions should flow to institutions, and the impact of any option on the beneficiaries of higher education – students and their families, the state and employers. These questions link to broader issues of the role of the state in higher education and the balance between central control and market influences.

Over the past decade the range of possible options for funding higher education has hardly changed. The key choice is between a

---

2 House of Commons (2001), Education and Employment Committee Fourth Report: 'Higher Education: Access'.

publicly funded system and one in which public and private funds are combined.

Some argue that the case for funding entirely from the public purse is weakened when the rationale for other forms of contribution is examined. Thus, for example, individuals make significant gains from higher education through higher average lifetime earnings, lower risks of unemployment, and a greater probability of finding a new job if made unemployed. Hence, they argue, students should bear the full cost of their higher education supported by income-contingent loans at favourable rates or by receiving support from scholarships.

In practice there are hardly any universities anywhere that rely either exclusively on public funding or exclusively on funding by present or past beneficiaries. A mix of the two is almost universal.

The Funding Options Review set out the spectrum of options for meeting the additional £900 million funding requirement by considering both public and private contributions to higher education and the various combinations of these. The review distinguished eight funding options and assessed them against a range of criteria, the top three of which were:

(a) Additional funding for institutions

Will the option provide institutions with additional core funding to maintain or improve the level of funding per student at the 2000/01 level in real terms and meet the additional funding requirement? Will the funding be truly additional or will it be offset by reductions in existing taxpayer support?

(b) Quality of the student experience

Will the option contribute to maintaining and enhancing the quality of teaching and learning? Are additional funds generated by the option likely to be available to enhance teaching and support infrastructure investment as opposed to being tied to specific initiatives? Will increased purchasing power in the hands of students create greater incentives for institutions to improve their teaching performance?

(c) Social inclusion

Will the option assist or hinder an increase in the participation of people from the lower socio-economic groups? What impact will it have on the financial calculations of these individuals and their families? Is the likely size of the future debt burden a disincentive to participation?

Four of the eight options were deemed to meet these criteria, particularly the crucial test of raising new money to meet the funding requirement if the right assumptions were made about the levels of public and private contributions. The four options were:

(i) Increased public funding

The required increase would be met from public funds, raised by general taxation, through an increase in the block grant funding for teaching from the higher education funding councils using the current funding approach. Thus this option would include the current student-number-based, subject-banded block grants from the funding councils, but at increased levels. Means-tested fee contributions would be maintained at their present levels in real terms. The current system of income-contingent loans for student maintenance with repayments through the tax system would be retained. The option could be modified to make grant support available, beyond that now proposed through Opportunity Bursaries for students from the poorest families and/or to increase the proportion of the loan that is means tested.

(ii) Market fees

The funding requirement would be met through differential fees paid directly to institutions. The current student-number-based, subject-banded block grants from the higher education funding councils would be retained at their present level. At least three types of fee differentiation would be possible – by subject cost, by prospective rate of return to the individual (as in the Australian funding system), and by deregulation. Deregulation could either involve 'top-up fees' or reductions in fees for subjects where recruitment was difficult – hence the use of the term 'market fees'. To enable students to pay fees the option would need to be accompanied by institutional funded scholarships for the poorest and publicly provided income-contingent loans for the remainder. As with Option (i) it could be combined with the current or a modified system of income-contingent loans for student maintenance.

(iii) Graduate income-contingent contributions

The current system of means-tested fees would be replaced by a system of capped income-contingent contributions paid by graduates after the completion of their courses. The loss by institutions of the current up-front means-tested fee contributions would need to be compensated by increased public funding. Such a system will be implemented in Scotland for Scottish-domiciled and EU students from September 2001, based on decisions by the Scottish Executive in response to the Cubie Report.[3]

Cubie recommended that an endowment fund should support institutions as well as students, while the Executive decided to give priority to the latter. However, in the option proposed here graduate contributions would form a second stream of funding for teaching to meet the funding requirement. Publicly funded income-contingent loans would be available to graduates to meet their contributions. As with Options (i) and (ii) this option could be combined with the current income-contingent loan system for student maintenance or a modified system.

(iv) Institutional endowment

Institutions would receive on submission of an acceptable proposal a one-off endowment from public funds to replace their current block grants from the funding councils for teaching and the public contribution to fees. This is essentially current Conservative Party policy. The endowments could come from securitisation of the student loan book, and/or from public funds. If the endowment came from public funds it could be argued that this option is simply replacing an expected flow of future grants with an immediate single block grant. It could, however, offer institutions more autonomy in the investment and spending of their funds than the

---

3   Independent Committee of Inquiry into Student Finance (2000) (the 'Cubie Report'), *Student Finance: Fairness for the Future*, Edinburgh.

current arrangements, though this would depend on the nature of the regulatory regime adopted. Although the Conservatives have indicated that they do not support fee deregulation, thus removing many of the potential benefits of the proposal, this option could be combined with Options (ii) or (iii) above.

It was not the intention of the Funding Option Review to identify a single preferred option. Rather its task was to lay out the range of options and the advantages and disadvantages of each. How the higher education system is funded in the future is ultimately a political decision. This fact was amply demonstrated at the time of the Dearing Report[4] when the government immediately announced a new and different system from that proposed by Dearing. Universities UK is keeping all the options on the table and continuing to promote a robust and evidence-based discussion of them. This includes the market fees option, even though all the main political parties have ruled them out.

The Funding Options Review provides a sound basis for preparations for the next spending review, expected in 2002. The role of Universities UK in this will be twofold:

- To demonstrate what has been achieved with the past public investment in higher education, i.e. to unpack the 'something for something' principle.
- To undertake research and analysis which will help to build the case for future increased investment in higher education.

---

4   National Committee of Inquiry into Higher Education (1997), *Higher Education in the Learning Society* (the 'Dearing Report'), HMSO, London.

A top priority will be building the case for increased investment in the teaching infrastructure. This means investment in buildings and equipment, including information technology, and also the staffing base of universities. Other priorities will be:

- funding to deliver the government's social inclusion agenda, particularly identifying the real cost of attracting and retaining people from disadvantaged backgrounds;
- the need for any further expansion to be fully funded;
- further investment in so-called third mission funding, which has brought benefits at the interface between universities and business and the community;
- continued investment in research, particularly the research infrastructure, in order to consolidate the funding gains made in the previous spending review;
- addressing the costs of implementing legislative requirements, particularly the Disability Discrimination Act and equal pay for work of equal value.

An increasing proportion of the UK electorate has had some experience of higher education. Full-time students are now, like their part-time and overseas counterparts, paying customers with means-tested contributions to tuition fees amounting to some £400 million per annum in England by 2003/04. There is thus an increasing emphasis on students as consumers making informed choices and seeking value for money for the investment that they have made.

This serves to emphasise the important and symbiotic relationship between institutions and their students. Without adequately supported students universities cannot do their job. The conditions need to be right to attract students, including those from disadvantaged backgrounds, to university. In this the nature and level of the student support package is crucial. Students need to have adequate time to study and be free from excessive worries about having enough money to live on. There is a gap in current knowledge about the impact of the new funding arrangements on students, particularly in terms of perceptions of debt. For this reason Universities UK is conducting a major research project into this issue. Moreover, students need to be taught by well-motivated staff in well-constructed buildings and well-provided libraries, lecture rooms and laboratories. Equipment needs to be in good repair and fit for its purpose. This in turn brings us back to the question of who pays for a high-quality, socially inclusive and competitive higher education system.

The shift in the balance of funding between the state and individuals will increasingly have electoral implications which will serve to keep higher education on the political agenda. There is every reason to believe that positive benefits will flow from this.

For its part the government, of whatever political persuasion, will need to demonstrate that the financial contributions made by students are genuinely additional and not a substitute for public funding. It will need to match its aspirations for higher education, in helping to deliver government priorities for social inclusion and a competitive knowledge-based economy, with adequate funding. In this, international comparisons will play a part as evidence already suggests that, after excluding research expenditure, the UK's level of investment per student is low compared to many of its principal competitors. The government will need to justify its accountability regimes and to respond to demands for red tape to be cut so that funding for universities' core business of teaching students and of research is maximised.

For their part universities will need to be even more sensitive and responsive to the needs of students. We may consider that the government and individuals derive a good deal from higher education, but universities will need to constantly convince others of this and produce evidence to support it. There will continue to be an emphasis on providing transparent and reliable public information for students and other stakeholders. This will need to cover the full range from input through to retention and employability measures.

Universities UK, in partnership with others, will be able to play a key role in developing robust evidence-based analysis which can be used to influence key decision-makers. We can help to make the case for future investment in universities. We can campaign for the changes needed to establish the right balance between accountability for public funds and the freedom universities need to achieve real change in the social composition of their intakes, to innovate and take the risks necessary to remain globally competitive, and to continue to play a vital part in fostering the values of a cohesive, democratic and pluralist society.

4 THE COLLAPSE OF THE ACADEMIC IN BRITAIN
Kenneth Minogue

The fate of the academic world in Britain

No one doubts that British universities have been transformed since 1960. Should we regard this as a triumph of democratisation, in which the riches of the centuries have become available to (nearly) all? Or should we rather consider it as the collapse of an academic culture? My view is that we are dealing with collapse. No doubt I exaggerate somewhat, but there's nothing like a bit of exaggeration to clarify the issues.

In 1960 Britain could boast a small but distinguished set of academic institutions respected the whole world over. By the end of the century, a rather different thing called 'higher education' was central to the country's prosperity, taking almost half the youth of the country under its wing. Meanwhile, the academic, as a distinct province of civil society, survived only in the interstices of the new creation. The story is a model of how independent institutions can be reduced to mere instruments of national policy. And like most of history's disasters, it was largely done with the best of intentions.

As far back as the 1920s, British governments had recognised that universities could usefully be supported, and did so through a 'hands off' mechanism called the University Grants Committee (UGC). It worked in part through local authorities, and grants were made to cover a five-year period, allowing universities to plan ahead. This admirable restraint even survived World War II, when governments had again experienced the thrill of wartime control over society. But state subsidy is always dangerous: it is the first step towards state control. In the late 1950s, spending money on further education was coming to be seen as the necessary condition of rising commercial prosperity. A commission was established, and the Robbins Report of 1963 recommended vast expansion. In fact, so great was the consensus on its desirability, the expansion had already begun. By 1972, the 17 universities of 1945 had become 45. Thirty polytechnics were also soon flourishing.

By the 1980s, the UGC was no more, and the Ministry of Education, flaunting its democratic accountability for the way public money was spent, was doling out cash (on an annual basis) through Funding Councils. By the 1990s, universities were unmistakably merely a part of a comprehensive state system of instruction for those above eighteen years of age. They were inspected and controlled as such.

It was not only the finances which had been transformed. The student of earlier times, who could exhibit the initiative to make his own contribution to the intellectual life of the university, was largely replaced by a young person who had to be (such at least was the assumption of those engaged in 'academic audits') provided with the exact materials needed to succeed in examinations. Universities even lost their control over whom they might choose to admit as students. Additional funds were promised to universities that complied with the current plans – for example, admitting more poor, ethnic and female students so that their 'representation' in higher education would correspond to their proportions in society as a whole. Ability was being replaced by quota. In February 2001, the House of Commons Education Select Committee was, in the wake of the Chancellor of the Exchequer's rebuke to Oxford University for not admitting a particular student, recommending a substantial increase in the premium paid to universities for admitting students from poor socio-economic backgrounds.[1] Funds for research had been centralised, and academics had to apply to official committees in order to get the money needed for research.

Subsidy and democratisation were thus two of the processes which led to the collapse of the academic in Britain during the second half of the 20th century, and it is significant that both governing parties exhibited the same relentless drive to dominate. The Department of Education was itself an independent player in the story. Efficient administration strongly suggests tidiness and centralisation. Centralisation of power is extremely difficult to reverse. Power is more easily acquired than relinquished.

The real character of the academic

What I must now do is justify my assertion that the academic has *collapsed* in Britain. This is a dramatic way of putting it, and many would reject the judgement by glorying in the thought that nearly half of British youth is now involved in 'higher education'. We need not doubt that a lot of useful work is done in this area. It is not, however, academic. What is the character of academic life?

Scholarship and academic inquiry are among the many independent activities of which society is constituted, and these activities, as traditions over time, 'take people up', as it were. We

---

1   *The Times*, 6 February 2001.

commonly think, say, that Hobbes took up philosophy, Isaac Newton physics, Purcell music, and this does indeed correspond to one aspect of our complex world. But we may also say that the tradition of philosophical thinking, as found in the books and conversation of the world in which Hobbes lived, took *him* up, as physics took up Newton and music Purcell, all according to their tastes and capacities. Such established traditions generally operate through institutions which formalise the way in which these activities are carried on. Traditions of this kind are independent forms of enterprise, and any society will be a bundle of such things. They always subserve various outside purposes, but many of them also have a certain disinterestedness, an independent purchase upon our loyalties.

These activities are part of the vast complex we may call 'society'. They fit into a kind of harmonious order, but they may also find themselves in conflict with each other. Governments, for example, would like political philosophers to give an account of political reality sympathetic to the current regime, and in defying this demand Hobbes thought it wise to get out of England during the Civil War, his independence being under threat. Religions have at various stages sought to dominate the conclusions of scientists and philosophers, while innovators in music may find themselves in conflict with popular taste for repeating nice familiar tunes.

I take the academic world to be one of these autonomous traditions. It is a kind of formalised curiosity or wonder, and it has created its own forms and procedures in Western societies ever since the twelfth-century Renaissance. It is a valuable fact of life that each European country has its own version of this tradition. Generally, the academic tradition will be found in universities, where the sustaining of scholarship has been formalised and the transmission of a certain kind of cultivation arranged for students. Yet like all traditions, the academic has its ups and downs. The dons who inhabit universities may become torpid and merely exploitative of their sinecures, and, especially at these times, the academic impulse will sometimes flourish as much outside the university as within it. Just such a flourishing took place in the international republic of scientists and scholars in the seventeenth century. Again, universities had to be comprehensively reformed in the nineteenth. But we may define the academic tradition, however it expresses itself, as the cultivation of scholarship and inquiry distinct from and often critical of the beliefs and activities of the rest of society. The academic world, in other words, is a special kind of place, marked off by rituals and commonly by distinctive dress of its own. Practical men, quite rightly, deride as 'academic' the carefulness about exact truth which commonly marks the don.

So long as they were regarded as amiably useless, and largely sustained themselves by the endowments they had inherited and the fees their students paid, universities were safe from the ambitions of other parts of society. Here was a world of 'remote ineffectual dons thinking about everything from black dwarfs to Linear B, from the aesthetic qualities of Jane Austen to the reasons for trade cycles'. And the significant thing was that this very freedom from outside pressure was often the source of their creativity. Advances in pure mathematics and logic could turn out to be remarkably useful, though no one would ever have funded research in them. An interest in old garbage turned out to reveal prehistory. These nice, harmless, unhurried, unharassed institutions in Britain notched up an admirable score of Nobel prizes and similar baubles, but their value also lay in the respect they enjoyed in the international field of the academic. And much of their value depended on managing to keep governments and ministers from exploiting them.

No real institution can avoid acquiring contingent encrustations. In Britain, the universities of Oxford and Cambridge were both academically admired, and socially grand. They were also finishing schools for the rich. Other pedagogic institutions envied them, and some dreamed of imitating their practices, appropriating their titles, enjoying their leisure and even (ridiculous as it seems today) cutting themselves in on their salary levels. Polytechnics particularly complained that this situation was iniquitous, and that they were on the wrong side of what they called the 'binary line'. They demanded 'parity of esteem'. The very name 'university' had a cachet everyone sought. Governments love 'underdogs'. It allows them to manage social esteem, and to enjoy the popularity that comes from including the excluded. And this can be done, apparently at no cost, by inflation. Names can be devalued as easily as currencies. Hence the administrative centralisations of the 1980s reached their culmination when, in 1993, the polytechnics and other colleges instantly became universities, by official fiat. A comprehensive system of higher education had been created out of the flexible and diverse set of institutions Britain had sustained before 1960.

The techniques of subversion

The practical criteria of usefulness and relevance are particularly deadly to academic (as to artistic) life. They obliterate both the sense of the past and the flight of imagination. Fashion rules, and is always at the mercy of current political attitudes. In modern

Britain, universities were by virtue of their prestige obviously chickens crying out to be plucked. No aspirant reformer could fail to notice indolence, pedantry and other academic vices that are regarded in bureaucratic terms as waste. All that had in the past protected universities from destruction by reform was a certain kind of mysterious prestige. The threat was a functional view of society in which value was contribution to some notional common good.

What contribution did universities make to society? Simple minds found it plausible to say that they had always educated people for useful careers. In the past, it had been careers in the Church, but times had changed, and now the business of universities was to act as the cognitive powerhouse society needed to compete in the modern world. Universities, like everyone else, must change with the times. I apologise to the sophisticated reader for sullying his mind with these gruesome simplicities, but the truth must be told that even some dons actually believed this kind of thing. Connoisseurs of the march of servility will also recognise here a familiar rhetorical device. Those who propose to destroy an institution begin by distorting its history.

The university as an independent element in civil society thus found itself at the mercy of democracy, alias the government. The academic pursuit of truth got itself entangled with the commercial pursuit of prosperity. The university as an amiable backwater diffusing its civilising restraint on whatever was the contemporary nonsense became the technological powerhouse every state needed. Governments set up research councils which would guide scholars in making themselves useful. No doubt much of this was benign, but it expressed the Bolshevik illusion that modern people were ready to make everything conform to a plan of betterment. The result is to lock academics into whatever is the current paradigm. It destroys creativity and innovation, though the hubris of the state now promises to 'manage' even these things.

The consequences of democratisation

The switch from talking of 'universities' to talking of 'higher education' gives the rhetorical key to the subversion of universities. Going to a university is conditional on having the capacity to participate actively in the kind of thinking and inquiry that scholarship and research require. A 'right' to higher education is a demand to be given a certain quantum of more or less unconditional academic attention. There can be no unconditional right to go to a university. Teaching in universities is quite different from the kind of teaching people are familiar with in schools. A university student is a kind of apprentice. He is in fact assumed to be *already* educated and therefore to be academically self-moving. He or she should be able to make his own way in cultivating a subject, and the relatively formal disciplines of lectures and examinations are no substitute for the essential business of going on educating oneself. The thing called 'higher education', by contrast, is the processing of young people so that they acquire such skills as are currently valued. The new system of 'academic audits' mechanised undergraduate teaching, and a similar homogenisation has been promoted by the research councils in graduate studies. Independent reflection gets crowded out.

Democratisation, like 'inclusion', is an attack on the 'élitism' thought to characterise universities. Elitism reveals itself either by high standards or institutional barriers. Groucho Marx, it will be remembered, would not join any club prepared to admit him, but the *demos* generally lacks this delicate sensibility. Wherever its nose is pressed against the glass, it seeks to enter. And it will be (briefly) grateful to the government that removes the barriers to doing so.

This is why the standard demands for competence in Latin, mathematics or foreign languages were dropped as the 1960s advanced. New subjects also had to be found for sustaining the attention of young persons often unequipped with a passion for cognitive challenge. Intellectualised political enthusiasms, such as Marxism and feminism, came to be accepted as if they were legitimate academic conclusions of inquiry. Indignation at supposed oppressions was an easy device for capturing student attention. Politicising subjects, and then turning the politics into melodrama, however, is rather like being trapped in an endless murder mystery in which the murderer is known from the start. It is pointless. Democratisation soon equipped every 'minority' with an academic parody of its own. Reasons were soon found for making the study of comics or journalism no less worthy than Shakespeare or Old Norse. The standpoint of the universal, hitherto the essence of a university, gave way to a kind of tribalism. I cannot put the point more tersely than Bradford P. Wilson of the National Association of Scholars in the United States:

> One's race, one's sex, one's 'culture' are, in the context of the ends of liberal education, caves from which education is meant to be an ascent. It is a betrayal of the idea of the university to engage in recruitment practices, organize extracurricular student life, and open the curriculum to innovations that have the explicit goal of confirming students in their origins rather than giving them the

intellectual depth by which they can transcend those origins.[2]

The fate of academic research

The idea of the university and the idea of higher education are thus not only distinct but in many respects diametrically opposed. This can be seen in the way in which the British government has nationalised research. There are four research councils, and I only encounter one of them. But if the rest are as bad, then academic independence is indeed at an end. The Economic and Social Research Council publishes a regular account of what it has been up to, a document full of managerial jargon about policy formation, guidelines and targets, improving the quality of research, and so on. A recent issue is focused on the welfare state, and reverentially reports some remarks made by the Prime Minister, Tony Blair. '... I believe it is vital that Britain's intellectual community is full and constructively engaged in the Government's agenda and priorities. Our jobs and perspectives may be different but I believe our goals are shared.'[3] Stalin could hardly have put it better. The servility of universities, at least in aspiration, is complete.

How did this happen? The causes are, of course, complex, and some of them will be found in the deeper rhythms of our civilisation. But what is most remarkable is the supine response of the dons themselves. Some reasons for this, however, are unmistakable. In the first place, dons were bribed in the 1960s by being

---

2   'Reflections on the Postmodern University' in *NAS*, the newsletter of the National Association of Scholars, Vol. 11, No. 1, 2000.

3   Quoted in 'New Society or New Individualism', *Social Science, News from the ESRC*, January 2001, Issue 47, p. 7.

given a lot of money and many opportunities for power and promotion. Whole new empires in glamorous new universities opened up, and it was flattering to the average don to think that his work was of national importance. By the time the screws began to tighten in the 1970s, dons were caught in a mindset of their own making. They had accepted the idea that universities were functional to the nation, and in all consistency they had to take the rough with the smooth. That is part of the reason why they now find themselves miserably enmeshed in bureaucratised impotence.

One thing this elementary corruption cannot conceal is, of course, a certain lack of courage in standing up to ministries that disposed of all the cash and most of the power. Choosing freedom has its costs, and the academic berths, bad as they got, were much more comfortable than the world outside.

But the most fundamental cause of the collapse was, I suggest, the failure of a generation of careerist university teachers to understand what made them a distinct vocation. The minds of many had been corroded by a generalised political allegiance which told them that their highest duty was not to the academy but to the job of perfecting society. The disinterested pursuit of truth seemed small beer in comparison; indeed, the simpler ones thought that only a perfected society would at last allow truth to flow freely.

Would it have made any difference if they had better understood their own vocation? I think it would, but self-understanding itself raises difficulties. Just as Polemarchus in *The Republic* has a pretty good formula for justice, but could not really understand the formula itself, so university teachers in the 1960s commonly thought that the essence of the academic was criticism. But 'criticism' happens to refer to anything from appreciating a poem to the ejaculation 'yuk!'. In the confused period as expansion began, a whole generation of Marxist students abruptly surfaced declaring: 'the essence of the academic is criticism, and we are being critical – of society. Join our crusade, or you betray your integrity.' This grisly misunderstanding persuaded some academics, and silenced many others. It was a form of moral dogmatism which with astonishing speed performed a somersault. One form of criticism – discrimination – was violently extruded from the university. It turned out that criticism must only apply to a schedule of approved objects: students must not be criticised for ignorance, nor popular materials on the ground of banality. The slippery term 'criticism' turned out to be a bridge by which the university as the custodian of demanding standards of excellence slid into a promiscuous policy of 'anything goes'. And this switch was paralleled in a virtual collapse of formality in universities. Dons no longer wore academic robes, and their students, usually lounging around in jeans and sneakers, did not bother with ties.

The academic world as a mysterious realm

Harold Macmillan once remarked that the real thing one got out of going to Oxford was being able to detect when a chap was talking rot. The current Prime Minister (as we have seen) talks 'rot' a great deal of the time – a judgement agreed right across the political spectrum. But what he has to say also resonates with 'vibes' (the vulgar term is unavoidable) which appeal to thousands of those emerging from the system of higher education, much of which might well be defined as induction into the 'higher rot'.

This is why it is dangerous to identify the essence of the academic with an abstraction such as 'criticism'. University inquiry had the aspect of a craft, and, like all crafts, it was a mystery. Mystery is what gives a special significance to materials; it is what helps to turn mere information into knowledge by locating it in a world of inquiry. It cannot be contained in a formula. Mystery cannot survive intimacy and matiness; it requires a certain distance and formality. It certainly excludes those who cannot follow the argument. It requires the submission of an adept.

The great enemy has been journalism, along with its academic beachhead, popularisation. This appeals to a vanity of knowledge-ability, and generates excitement not by cultivating a mystery of understanding, but by purporting to conduct us behind the scenes – behind those boring technicalities – in order to get to the heart of a matter which does not have a heart. Oxford made A. J. P. Taylor a pariah because he would pontificate on anything for a dozen guineas. The eccentric F. R. Leavis loathed the intellectual journals of the metropolis to an absurd extent – but he instinctively recognised (especially with a subject such as English literature) that to dilute the academic would reduce his subject to journalism, or alternatively incite it to the ecstasies of scholasticism and obscurity by which it now tries to present itself as hard knowledge.

The decline of the Anglican Church is an object lesson in the fate of traditions that give up their mystery – which is also a form of self-limitation. To become involved in the mystery of a craft is to embrace limitation, to become, from an external point of view, rather absurd. Today, this kind of creative limitation often finds it difficult to survive against a matey, inclusive world whose informalities of dress and speech signal that we are all the same clay. We become locked into a tyrannical normality from which it is hard to escape and whose range the media constantly determine. In this world, there is always a history man being intimate with his students down in the bar, and village atheists and champagne (or, more exactly, sparkling Chardonnay) socialists set the tone. Making 'knowledge' accessible to all merely reduces the wonder of science or philosophy to the commonplaces of the textbook.

So: the academic has collapsed. It survives, no doubt, in the interstices of many universities, and there remain plenty of able and alert dons who do know what it is all about. But all too many now take their cue from the 'academic audit', and write formularised articles for professional journals. In the seventeenth century, the cultivation of inquiry migrated to the world of the independent scholar, and it has been suggested that 'think tanks' might take up the academic role today. They do many admirable things, but they certainly do not sustain academic inquiry.

Here, then, is one saga in the creation of our servile state, which may be defined as the subordination of independent institutions to, as Mr Blair puts it, the priorities of the state. The various ministers who have presided over this process – Shirley Williams, Kenneth Baker, Kenneth Clarke, David Blunkett, *et al.* – were all, as the Ministry of Education poured out their hundreds upon hundreds of pages of laws and regulations, animated by the best of intentions, but they have (as Elie Kedourie memorably put it) turned diamonds into glass.[4] Animated by an egalitarian hatred of élitism, they have destroyed the reflective quality of English academic life. Like every other independent tradition, the academic is now being squeezed dry by the government. The dark, moist, untapped places where new things grew unhurried by politicians have all been taken over and put to work. We are living off the creativity of past generations and replacing very little. The materials

---

4   See Elie Kedourie, *Diamonds into Glass: the Government and the Universities*, Centre for Policy Studies, 1988.

for recreating the academic world have not yet been entirely destroyed but they are running low. And the real danger may very well be that this collapse of the academic might itself come to be recognised, in the current public idiom, as a 'problem', with the government itself trying to provide the solution. That would be the ultimate disaster. As the merchants of Paris are reported to have growled, when Colbert offered them help to increase the mercantilist power of France: *laissez-nous faire.*

5 UK UNIVERSITIES AND THE STATE: A FAUSTIAN BARGAIN?
Tony Dickson

The start of the new millennium brought with it some strange portents for the university sector in the UK. In 2000 the decision by an Oxford college not to offer a university place to Laura Spence, a pupil at a state school on Tyneside, despite her possession of outstanding A-level grades, was the subject of a national debate. The then Secretary of State for Education, David Blunkett, took this decision as evidence of the unwillingness of certain 'élite' universities to embrace the government's agenda for widening access and participation in higher education. As a result, government funding was found to persuade some of these universities to offer activities such as summer schools which might encourage a larger number of able pupils from state schools to apply to them. A new performance indicator was also introduced for universities to track the numbers and proportions of applications and acceptances from state school pupils.

The same year saw the national organisation of university vice-chancellors rename itself unimaginatively but descriptively as Universities UK in order to have a more effective brand for its marketing and lobbying activities. It also agreed to its Chief Executive, Diana Warwick, accepting appointment as a working peer for the Labour government in the House of Lords, despite Universities UK having a primary role as an independent lobby for higher education in the UK. Following a similar line of argument, Universities

UK published early in 2001 a study that it had commissioned on options for securing greater funding for the university sector to begin to rectify the funding crisis that it had been describing for at least five years.[1] The study outlined a series of options, most of which would involve a greater contribution from private funding. Universities UK refused to indicate a preference for any one of these options on the grounds that a general election was imminent and that this was therefore the wrong time to bring pressure to bear on the government! Alongside this decision, the government quango which funds English universities, the Higher Education Funding Council for England (HEFCE), announced that it had asked at least six universities to submit 'Recovery Plans' since they were facing major financial difficulties arising from their failure to recruit their targeted student numbers.

How are we to read these signs and to make sense of what they tell us? The answer lies in understanding the nature of the relationship which has been constructed over the last 40 years between the university sector and the state in the UK. Put simply, the development of this relationship over that period, though not always through consistent and deliberate intent on either side, has ensured that the university sector is now one of the last semi-nationalised sectors of the British economy. That is, it is seen by government as being a part of the public sector and as a legitimate instrument of social policy which can be steered in such a way as to support the short-term goals of a particular political administration. This article will argue that this position is a Faustian bargain which threatens the continued quality and prosperity of the UK

---

1   Universities UK (2001), *New Directions for Higher Education Funding* (the 'Taylor Report'), London.

university sector, and that the dependence of universities on the state must be changed by embracing different methods of funding and supporting the university sector.

Universities and the state

In order to look forward to new and better funding methods, it is necessary first briefly to note some of the signposts that have marked the development of the peculiarly British version of the state–university sector relationship. These would include as a starting point the interventions in education of the Labour governments of the 1960s as successive administrations looked for ways to modernise the economy and attack the skills and training deficits which were a feature of the postwar period. Thus, the creation of the polytechnics and the Open University can be seen as quite explicit attempts to increase the return on human capital from the Treasury perspective. It can also be seen to open up British society to a meritocratic and socially equitable future in which a much larger section of the population could gain access to higher education and acquire more relevant skills than those typically taught in traditional and élitist universities.

Later government interventions in higher education, although undertaken by different political parties, mostly drove farther down the road of greater corporatist control of universities. The University Grants Council was abolished in the 1980s as it was seen to be too much of an independent buffer between government and its expectations of the universities. The polytechnics were steered initially through a combination of national quangos (the National Advisory Board for funding, and the Council for National Academic Awards for course approvals and quality assurance) and regional planning through the local authorities. When the gathering tensions over diminishing the role of local government grew too acute, the polytechnics were 'freed' from local government control in 1989 and established as legally independent corporations but with funding channelled through a new national funding body, the Polytechnic and Colleges Funding Council (PCFC). This was a parallel body to the University Funding Council (UFC) which had replaced the UGC. Both these organisations were steered through an annual funding letter from the Secretary of State for Education, with government policy clearly spelled out in relation to deliverables from the higher education sector. In 1992, the binary line in higher education was abolished and a new unified sector was created by bringing together the universities and the polytechnics under a merged UFC and PCFC – the Higher Education Funding Council.

Two major points can be made about consistency of purpose by successive governments in relation to higher education during this period. The first is that a recurrent theme since the 1960s has been the relentless expansion of the sector. Although the rate of expansion has ebbed and flowed with economic cycles and the pressures on government funding, the system has nevertheless continued to expand so that less than 10 per cent of the school leaving population went into higher education in the 1960s, nearly 35 per cent entered in 2000, and the Prime Minister, Tony Blair, has declared a 50 per cent target as current government policy. Thus, while the rhetoric of Labour governments has often been focused on social inclusion as the justification for expansion, and that of Conservative governments has stressed the need for market skills, both have backed periods of major growth in higher education. However, since that period of expansion has also coincided with a time in which the performance of the British economy has often been moderate in international terms, the growth of the system has been accompanied by a relentless pressure on the unit of resource in higher education. The average unit of resource per student has fallen by 38 per cent since 1989, following a decrease of 20 per cent between 1976 and 1989.[2]

This policy has long-established origins. The polytechnic sector was created by a Labour government as a means of achieving cheaper growth in more vocationally relevant areas. When, in a later period, a Conservative government wished to drive growth within a difficult economic framework it established the PCFC in 1989 and gave its Chairman, Ron Dearing, an ex-Treasury civil servant, the task of finding an appropriate methodology. Aided by an enthusiastic and able Chief Executive, Bill Stubbs, the PCFC devised a growth methodology which combined a squeeze on the core funding of the polytechnics with an invitation to bid for additional student numbers at marginal pricing. In a cash-constrained environment, many institutions went for the short-term attractions of extra revenue for more students, even if it meant driving down the unit cost of education. For four years this methodology drove a massive and rapid expansion of the system. Many of the universities now facing 'Recovery Plans' can trace the roots of their current financial vulnerability to this 'dash for growth'. It is also an ironic consequence that the main architects of this strategy to cheapen the cost of provision, Ron Dearing and Bill Stubbs, subsequently both knighted for their contributions to government policy, were to re-emerge later in quite different roles in higher education. Bill Stubbs took the basic methodology to the further

---

2   *New Directions for Higher Education Funding*, op. cit., 10.

education sector as the first Chief Executive of the Further Education Funding Council (FEFC), with similar effects on reducing unit costs and increasing financial vulnerability in the sector, and then jumped over the wall to become Rector of the London Institute. Ron Dearing, having presided over the fastest reduction in unit costs in the history of higher education, was appointed in 1996 to head the Dearing Inquiry, which was established to analyse the funding crisis in the university sector![3]

If cheaper unit costs have been the first major plank of government policy in the last 40 years, especially since 1989, then the second has been the tendency to become more and more specific about the policy confines within which the university sector should operate. Close control was a feature of the polytechnic sector from its origins; the UGC was abolished when it became clear that it could not be relied on to act as an agent of government policy, and the directions of the Secretary of State to successor funding bodies have grown more detailed and explicit over the years. For example, HEFCE now routinely top-slices income from the government to hold back from universities until they can show that they have complied with a range of government directives on policy. These now include having explicit strategies for widening access and participation, HR (human relations) strategies which include performance-related pay and equal opportunities, demonstrating actions relevant to regional policy, and funding premiums for mature students and for recruiting students from particular postcodes (and from state schools). A plethora of performance indicators is now being produced to ensure that HEFCE (and the

3   National Committee of Inquiry into Higher Education (1997), *Higher Education in the Learning Society* (the 'Dearing Report'), HMSO, London.

government) can know that universities comply with this range of policy expectations.

Public funding and the university sector

It is this background of development since the 1960s which helps to explain how UK universities now find themselves seen by government as an implementation arm for their policy initiatives. It also explains why the Secretary of State and a number of his parliamentary colleagues felt justified in commenting on a student application decision by an Oxford college, why Universities UK do not think it strange to have their Chief Executive acting as a working Labour peer, and why they would refuse to comment on funding issues for fear of embarrassing the government close to a general election.

Yet, despite the apparent dissonance between this dependence on the state and the usual rhetoric of universities about their role as independent and detached critical agencies, their engagement in the pursuit of truth, and their research-based examination of the frontiers of knowledge, it is possible to argue that there is a sustainable case for a close relationship with the state if the results of that relationship are to underpin these aspects of universities and enable them to prosper. However, a cursory glance at the current state of UK universities suggests that they are not deriving too many obvious benefits from this relationship.

First, by their own admission, there is a persistent and long-term funding crisis in the university sector. The unit of resource has been decimated. Most universities operate with a year-on-year revenue surplus considerably below the 3 per cent of turnover that HEFCE recommends as a minimum. As a result the sector is undercapitalised and under-invested. Another way of saying this is to point to the fact that the UK government spends less on higher education as a proportion of GDP than most other OECD nations, and continues to have a comparatively low spend on non-military R&D. Second, the sector also is subject to what is arguably the most intrusive and expensive audit regime of any higher education system in the world. This includes internal and external financial audit as public sector organisations, HEFCE audit, QAA Subject Review and Continuation Audit, the TTA and OFSTED, and accreditation by a wide range of professional bodies. From the QAA alone derives an audit process which includes subject review, institutional review, overseas audits, subject benchmarks, programme specifications, and dozens of Codes of Practice to which all universities must show compliance. HEFCE itself recently estimated the cost of this set of overlapping audit processes as a minimum of £250 million per year for the sector. Furthermore, all universities are required to submit all their activities to these various audits, even those activities that are funded by other bodies and may take place outside the UK. This leads to the bizarre situation in which some universities derive less than 20 per cent of their total income from HEFCE but are nevertheless forced to account for all their activity in the same way.

The impact of the QAA regime in particular sparked a revolt early in 2001 led by the London School of Economics, in which a number of universities indicated that they were preparing to reject the right of QAA to inspect their provision. This stance was sufficient to persuade David Blunkett, then Education Minister, to announce a new 'light touch' inspection regime for those universities that had already produced good-quality outcomes from the existing system. This change of policy was announced before it had been discussed with the QAA itself. It remains to be seen whether it is sufficient to head off the threatened revolt.

Third, the effect of such onerous and conservative audit processes is to ensure that the whole sector is risk averse. The spectres of the Treasury, the National Audit Office and the Public Accounts Committee lurk behind any action taken by a university which may involve some element of risk. Enterprise and innovation might be said to be low on the list of characteristics which are encouraged by this regime. Fourth, at a time when globalisation is beginning to have real impacts on higher education, a sector which is undercapitalised, overly regulated and risk averse is not well placed to make major strategic choices about alliances, investments and joint ventures which may be required to move from acting historically as a UK-based SME (small and medium-sized enterprise) to creating a multinational education business.[4]

Finally, a government mindset which sees universities primarily as a means to achieve its policy objectives will inevitably undervalue the contributions that universities make to the national and local economies as businesses in their own right. That is, UK universities are now fairly substantial service-sector businesses with turnovers often of hundreds of millions of pounds and are direct employers of thousands of staff. The effects of universities on local economies have only recently been the subject of detailed analysis.[5] Furthermore, in addition to their direct economic effects,

---

4 Committee of Vice Chancellors and Principals (CVCP) and Higher Education Funding Council for England (HEFCE) (2000), 'The Business of Borderless Education: UK perspectives – analysis and recommendations', London.

5 Stone, I. (2000), 'Northumbria: Growing a First Class Business', Northumbria University, Newcastle-upon-Tyne, and University of Newcastle (1996), 'Universities and Economic Development: A Report to the DfEE', University of Newcastle, Newcastle-upon-Tyne.

universities are key contributors to cultural and social life through their involvement in institutions such as art galleries, theatres and museums, constitute the core of UK R&D capacity, and act as a major factor in inward investment decisions. Thus, compared with most other businesses of comparable size, they bring a great deal of added value to the country.

For all these reasons, there is little evidence that the particularly close relationship to the state offers much benefit to UK universities. Yet, despite an increasingly unsupportive environment over the last 30 years, British universities remain high-quality institutions when judged on comparative measures. Their research output on most quality indicators remains in the top echelons internationally across a range of subject areas. Graduate completion rates, at over 80 per cent, are only exceeded by Japan. After their US counterparts, the UK universities are the most popular destination for overseas students. The paradox of the current situation is the apparent indifference of successive UK governments to one of the few sectors of UK Ltd which, if judged on a range of international comparators, would be ranked as world class. It is the continuation of this eminence which is threatened by the relationship of the UK university sector to the state.

Private investment and university development

At the heart of this problem is the question of the long-term funding of universities in the UK. Put simply, it is difficult to see UK universities maintaining their quality position internationally with a declining unit of resource and inadequate investment, and whilst operating within an overly regulated and risk-averse environment. The most that the Labour government elected in 1997 promised was a slowing down of the rate of decrease of the unit of resource. Nor is it likely that any future government will change this position. The reasons for this lie in the nature of the processes of globalisation and their effects on higher education. In most countries we can identify a cycle of education investment and development that occurs at different speeds and with varied implementation arrangements but which nevertheless demonstrates a regular pattern. In this cycle, the state first invests in basic literacy and numeracy at the primary education level and parallels this with a cautious commitment to secondary schooling. The required length of secondary education is then gradually extended over time as skills development at higher levels becomes an imperative for economic development. In line with this cycle, enrolment in secondary education worldwide has expanded tenfold over the last 50 years – from 40 million in 1950 to 400 million in 2000.[6]

This investment pattern then eventually creates a growing demand for increased tertiary-level education in colleges and universities. Over the last 50 years, enrolments in tertiary education have increased fourteen-fold, from 6.5 million in 1950 to 88.2 million in 2000. This trend is likely to accelerate as the demands of what has been called 'the knowledge economy' impact globally. This is where the state begins to experience a major investment crisis. The unit of resource necessary for tertiary education is usually far higher than that at primary and secondary levels, and the demand for extra investment at tertiary level runs parallel to increasing demands for other forms of investment in social infrastructure, most obviously in health and social security provision. The most

---

6   'Investing in Education: Analysis of the 1999 World Education Indicators', OECD, 2000.

common response to this crisis is for the state to encourage a much greater investment by the private sector through tuition fees and/or private education provision. Worldwide, it is estimated that private investment accounts for 37 per cent of all education provision. This is reflected in higher education systems throughout the world with substantial and rapidly growing private-sector provision – in the US, most of South America, South-East Asia and China. However, at the tertiary level the UK is unusual in international terms in being at one end of the spectrum of the mix of public and private investment. There is still only one UK university that is fully privately funded – the University of Buckingham, created 25 years ago.

It is unlikely that this situation can last much longer. The universities themselves are becoming more vocal about the regulatory regime and the funding crisis and its consequences. The introduction of tuition fees has opened the door to private contributions to costs. The global pattern of education investment will increase the current pressures. The key issue is therefore how to identify ways in which to increase funding to UK universities so as to enable them to retain international competitiveness. A major part of the answer will lie in increasing private investment in the sector. It may be useful to review briefly some of the options for achieving this, together with the main arguments for and against them.

The Taylor Report, commissioned by Universities UK, in effect identified three major options through which more private funding might flow to universities. The first was by allowing differential (top-up) tuition fees whereby each university would be free to charge what it believed the market would bear. The Labour government currently sets a capped limit to such fees and insists that it apply uniformly. It indicated in 2001, in the run up to the general election, that it expected to maintain that stance if it were re-elected. The second option was graduate income contingent contributions (a graduate tax), through which individuals would repay part of their tuition costs after they had graduated and were earning above specified salary levels. This option could of course be combined with Option 1. Finally, it analysed an option outlined by the Conservative Party to create capital endowments for universities financed primarily through the continuing sale of public assets.

The Taylor Report analysed the pros and cons of each of these options but carefully avoided expressing a preference. Before addressing the general question of the arguments for or against encouraging greater private investment in the UK university sector it may be worthwhile to suggest a further and more radical option which might also encompass Options 1 and 2 from the Taylor Report. This would be to offer the opportunity to some or all UK universities to float as publicly owned companies with equity available to private and institutional investors. Not all universities might choose to do so, some preferring to remain primarily attached to core government funding, accepting the close policy guidelines that would accompany that route. In the case of those institutions which chose to go down the equity route, the government might decide to retain a 'golden share', as it did in the case of the privatisation of other previously nationalised assets. Through this device the government retains its position as the 'owner of last resort', giving it the opportunity to intervene in situations of crisis should it choose to do so. Thus, in the event of a university being faced with a budget deficit which might lead to closure, the government would still have a choice about whether to allow this or not.

The privatisation of particular universities could be handled in much the same way as that of previous sectors, such as the utilities, with major financial intermediaries preparing a prospectus based on a valuation of the various kinds of assets (physical and intellectual) of each university. A guide price for the share issue would thus be determined and tested in the market by its IPO. The proceeds of the flotation would then be available as an endowment and investment fund for the university, in return for a reduced call on government funding thereafter. Universities which emerged as public companies would be free to raise capital against their share and asset values (raising very interesting questions as to how both accountants and the stock market would value education businesses whose primary assets are in intellectual capital). They could choose to contract with government (through HEFCE) for student numbers funded by the state. HEFCE would set numbers, price, a capped fee level, and also define the audit and policy constraints that the university would accept as part of their contract. These would include quality assurance arrangements, targets for recruitment from state schools, and so on. Outside that contract, universities would be free to diversify their sources of income and charge whatever fees they regarded as appropriate. They could thus recruit other students, from the UK or elsewhere, who were prepared to pay these fees.

Other universities might prefer to adopt a role more clearly aligned to the state and the public policy obligations which go with that. This might include funding routed through the regional bodies, such as RDAs and Regional Assemblies, being created as part of the Labour government's commitment to greater devolution of power to regions. Over time, the government might decide to place a higher proportion of its funded student numbers in such universities if they were seen to be delivering more effectively on the social agenda outlined by the government. In return, these universities would accept a closer level of control and accountability from the relevant public-sector agencies.

The result of this kind of partial privatisation of the universities would be to liberalise a number of features of the current system. It would encourage greater diversity in the sector, with more choice for individual institutions to pursue a distinctive mission. New sources of capital and investment would be available to the sector. The government could target its funding more directly at institutions that could demonstrate their capability and willingness to deliver on its agenda. The breaking of the uniform hegemony of audit and regulation would encourage greater enterprise. Some universities would have more freedom to develop as global institutions.

Funding options and equity

However, there are various objections that have already been raised against any options to increase private funding in the UK university sector. These revolve mainly around two important issues. The first is the claim that a system with greater private funding will inevitably lead to a more élitist, less socially inclusive sector, excluding in particular individuals from poorer social backgrounds. The second argument is that, whether the route is differential tuition fees or private provision, one result will be greater inequality between universities and greater instability. Both arguments need to be addressed.

Social inclusion is a key issue in any society as access to education at all levels tends over time to have a strong correlation to later economic success. However, to suggest that this issue is an a priori barrier to a higher education sector with greater private funding neglects one very important fact about the current university system in the UK. This is that the present regime of almost exclusive public funding of universities has been an abject failure as a means of tackling unequal access to higher education. For example, in 1998/99 a person from the professional class had a 72 per cent chance of entering higher education, while somebody from an unskilled background had only a 13 per cent chance – almost a sixfold differential.[7] Allowing for the massive growth in HE places over the last 30 years, and changes in occupational categories, social class differentials in access to HE in the UK have not changed significantly over this period. A major reason for this is, of course, that the barriers which lie behind this inequality of access are erected much earlier in people's lives and relate to family background, employment status of parents, expectations and experiences in primary education, and so on. Thus, while there are clearly universities whose selection practices skew their student intake in favour of certain social groups, the net impact of these practices on equality of access is comparatively trivial.

It follows that any argument which implicitly posits a contrast between publicly funded (more inclusive) HE and privately funded (more unequal) HE is, in terms of UK experience to date, unsustainable in the abstract. In addition, one can point to examples such as the US higher education system as being one of the most inclusive in the developed world but containing major elements of private provision which have developed very effective arrangements to offer access to students from less privileged backgrounds. Universities like Harvard and Princeton offer extensive bursaries

---

7   *Social Trends 2000.*

and scholarships, based on endowment funding, to such students. To encourage similar provision in an amended UK system the government could make some fairly simple changes to taxation to stimulate individual and corporate donations to universities.

Finally, it is pertinent here to highlight another well-established feature of the UK university system. Research[8] has confirmed that being a graduate in the UK has a pronounced positive effect on the lifetime earnings of the individual as compared with non-graduates. Thus, since the system also acts primarily to give access to the sons and daughters of the professional classes, one effect of continued public funding is to give a massive subsidy to the careers of individuals who already by definition come from relatively privileged backgrounds. It is difficult to reconcile arguments of social equity with this position. Furthermore, a system with more mixed provision, and less dependent on public funding, would allow the government to target its student support more effectively on those who most need it.

The second major objection to a system with more private investment is that it would lead to greater inequality between universities, with some prospering and expanding whilst others struggle to attract students. In reply, two major points can be made. First, the current system of public funding already achieves these effects. In addition to the six universities whose plight requires them to produce 'Recovery Plans', most others are struggling to avoid a revenue deficit each year. Second, universities in the UK are already unequal in many respects, and it is explicit government policy to preserve such inequalities. Most obviously, the distribution of research funding by HEFCE through a cycle of

8   For example, National Committee of Inquiry into Higher Education, op. cit.

Research Assessment Exercises at five-year intervals is explicitly designed to ensure a highly skewed distribution of funding with a small number of universities monopolising the vast bulk of these funds. For example, in 2001 the ten most successful universities in the UK, in terms of securing research income, took 48 per cent of all HEFCE research income (out of almost £900 million), 53 per cent of research income from other external sources (out of £1.5 billion), and 51 per cent of the money for research infrastructure allocated by HEFCE (out of £600 million).[9] On top of this, the funding formula for teaching students at different universities allows a 10 per cent variation around a norm – enough to make a substantial difference to the overall budget of most universities.

Thus, those who would advocate a retention of the current system have to show either how the very obvious shortcomings of this system will be overcome within public funding constraints or why a system with a more diverse funding base would be worse. It is not immediately apparent what the basis for this case might be. It is true that a university sector with more varied funding streams, and in which at least some universities were more directly exposed to market forces, would lead to greater diversity of provision. However, given the comparative strengths of the UK university sector in international terms there are good grounds for believing that most institutions would find ways to flourish in a higher education context that is becoming rapidly more global.

---

9   Higher Education Funding Council for England (HEFCE) (2001), Analysis of 2001 financial forecasts and annual operating statements, www.hefce.ac.uk/pubs/hefce/2001

UK universities in a global economy

The peculiarly heavy reliance on public funding in the UK university sector can be seen to have led to the current funding crisis through which the universities find themselves increasingly unable to guarantee the quality of teaching and research that has established the UK as a world-class centre for higher education. The pattern of education growth which is being repeated throughout the world as globalisation impacts on development suggests that few governments will be able to afford the high levels of investment that a publicly funded higher education system demands. In the vast majority of cases encouragement of more private provision and investment through tuition fees will be a major response to this issue. The UK currently stands uneasily to one side of this trend.

Other features of globalisation will reinforce the need to move forward decisively if the UK university sector is not to experience a rapid process of international decline. These are the combined influences of the shift of the corporate sector into corporate learning as a core feature of the development of its human capital, the ability of many education providers to extend their delivery patterns internationally through a base of e-learning via the Internet, and the need for universities to create new strategic alliances if they wish to operate globally (even if only to protect their existing market share from new forms of provision). This situation is creating a fiercely competitive higher education marketplace at all levels for UK universities – regionally, nationally and internationally. In order to be able to compete effectively in this environment UK universities need the flexibility to move quickly, revenue funding that maintains quality, and the scope for investment in new forms of provision inside and outside the UK. At the moment, public funding results in inadequate financing, poor access to sources of capital investment, low levels of social equity, and major inequalities between universities.

The injection of private funding and provision outlined in this article is not suggested as an instant panacea for all these problems. It does, however, offer the prospect of a more diverse system, less regulation and more enterprise, a more targeted use of public funds to support those universities that define their primary mission in relation to national and/or regional policy needs, scholarships and bursaries to support able students from less privileged backgrounds, and a development route through which at least some UK universities might pursue a path to future international excellence. Those who would resist the logic of private investment in higher education should explain the alternatives through which these objectives might be achieved.

6 INVESTING IN PRIVATE HIGHER EDUCATION IN DEVELOPING COUNTRIES: RECENT EXPERIENCES OF THE INTERNATIONAL FINANCE CORPORATION

Jacob van Lutsenburg Maas[1]

The private sector has for centuries played a major role in the creation of higher education institutions throughout much of the world. Religious missionaries founded many of the private institutions that were created before the 20th century in today's 'developing countries'. The 20th century, on the other hand, witnessed a vast expansion of the role of the state in higher education in both the wealthier industrial countries as well as in the colonies that became independent countries beginning in mid-century. The state became the numerically dominant provider as well as the financier of higher education in all but a few countries. However, in the final decades of the century, as overall public expenditures in most developing countries surpassed fiscal and debt-service capacities, the state slowed its growth in the sector even while public demand for more higher education accelerated.

This divergence between state supply and social demand created an opening for the resurgence of private initiatives in higher education. In this latest phase, the private sponsorship of

---

1   The author retired in 2001 as the Lead Education Specialist of the International Finance Corporation. The judgements expressed in this article are those of the author and should in no way be attributed to IFC management or its member countries.

universities and other higher education institutions has come from a wide variety of owners. While new religiously affiliated institutions continue to come into being as before, wealthy families or individuals, affinity groups and corporations are also creating new institutions. By 1998 the International Finance Corporation[2] had commissioned a pre-investment study of the global education industry,[3] and began to make its first investments in private higher education in developing countries. Meanwhile capital markets in selected countries, such as South Africa, the United States and the United Kingdom, began to direct new investment funds into private, for-profit education companies operating in domestic markets. And by the year 2000, for-profit education companies began to look for larger markets abroad, including in developing countries where the great majority of the world's university-age population – and thus the greatest potential for market growth – resides.

But what is the public policy rationale for private investment in private universities in developing countries? First, not only is there the widespread scarcity of available public funds to meet rising demand already noted. In addition, there is increased aware-

2　The IFC is the member institution of the World Bank Group dedicated to investing directly in private organisations implementing capital investment projects in developing and transition economies. Although its member governments own IFC, it invests without any form of government guarantee. In contrast, the World Bank itself provides concessional or semi-concessional loans to member governments of developing countries, or to government-owned corporations with a government guarantee.

3　A British consortium involving the Institute of Economic Affairs, the University of Manchester and Nord Anglia, a listed education company, carried out the study. It led to a monograph by the consortium leader: James Tooley (1999), *The Global Education Industry: Lessons from Private Education in Developing Countries*, IEA in association with IFC, London.

ness that public-sector institutions tend to lack incentives to adopt technological innovations as rapidly as is common in the private sector, where competitive pressures often force the adoption of new technologies. Thirdly, while basic education is generally viewed as providing significant 'public goods' through diffusion of basic literacy, numeracy and social skills, it is commonly observed that higher education deals largely in 'private goods', as evidenced by the significantly higher salaries commanded in the labour market by those with higher education qualifications. Fourthly, in terms of social equity, it is widely recognised in low-income, developing countries that almost all of the poor have fallen off the education 'ladder' well before reaching the age of admission to higher education. Since those entering higher education usually come from upper- or upper-middle-income groups, it is difficult to justify spending scarce public resources subsidising higher education when so many of the poor have not completed, or perhaps even begun, their basic schooling.

The recent opening of higher education to private investment is taking place against a backdrop of the Asian crisis of the late 1990s and a consequent greater reluctance by private investors in general to take large exposures in markets where political and economic turmoil sometimes appear chronic. So are conditions for investing in higher education in developing countries favourable and are there enough 'bankable' institutions and projects to attract private capital to these far-flung new markets? There are no easy answers yet to these valid questions. However, it is instructive to look at the early experiences of the International Finance Corporation, which has pioneered investments in this area.

The IFC's record is still very brief; it made its very first, small investment in education in 1995 and approved its first investment in a university in 1998. As of June 2001 IFC had approved investments in (a) nine universities, (b) two specialised post-secondary training centres for information technology and fire safety in West Africa, and (c) two student loan programmes in South Africa and India. These are summarised below.[4]

Universities

In May 1998 the IFC approved a US$22 million loan to the Universidad de Belgrano in Buenos Aires, Argentina, its first to a university. Like all private universities in Argentina, and as required by law, UB is constituted as 'not for profit', requiring it to reinvest its surpluses into the organisation. It is almost exclusively dependent for revenue on tuition fees from over 10,000 students. It was recognised that competition among private universities in Argentina had been increasing ever since a reform-minded government had begun relaxing restrictions on the creation of private universities in the early 1990s. UB offers technical, undergraduate and graduate degree programmes in many disciplines. The project involved: (a) the construction and furnishing of a 28,000-square-metre building to increase and modernise instructional facilities, (b) replacement of expensive existing medium-term with long-term credit, and (c) the reorganisation of a student loan programme which was burdened by bad debts. IFC worked closely with UB over a two-year period in an attempt to rein in operating

4   Information on IFC-approved investments can be obtained from the IFC website: http://wbln0018.worldbank.org/IFCExt/spiwebsite1.nsf/$$Search?Openform. Or go to IFC's home page, http://www.ifc.org/ , click on 'Projects and Policies' and then on 'IFC Project Documents Database', then fill in the form to bring up links to a Summary of Project Information (SPI) per project.

costs and improve corporate governance. However, owing to heightened competition from other private universities, UB proved unable to maintain enrolment levels, leading to a mutual decision to cancel the loan. Some immediate lessons learned from the experience are included in the issues section below.

IFC approved a US$9 million loan to Universidad Torcuato Di Tella, also in Buenos Aires, in January 1999. UTDT's offerings are focused on a set of fields where it has built a strong reputation: economics, business, international studies, political science and law. The investment project would implement UTDT's plan to grow its enrolments from 884 in 1998 to 1,900 by 2005. The signing of loan documents was delayed until October 2000 owing to significant regulatory obstacles in taking title to land and a government sanitary works building which UTDT purchased through a competitive bidding process, as well as delays in construction bidding. The university is performing well, although disbursement of the loan has been delayed.

In August 2000 IFC approved a US$5 million loan for Universidad de Montevideo in Uruguay. UM offers undergraduate and graduate degree programmes in economics, business administration and law, supplemented by an active programme of executive courses and seminars and other adult education programmes. The IFC loan supports a project which (a) expands UM's classroom facilities and library, (b) refinances expensive medium-term debt and (c) creates a student loan programme to be implemented under sound commercial principles by a banking partner, Banco Montevideo. The project will help enrolment grow from 1,500 students in 1999 to about 3,000 in 2006. The IFC loan was signed and first disbursement occurred in December 2000.

A US$7 million loan for Universidad Peruana de Ciencias

Aplicadas, SAC, in Lima, Peru, was approved by the IFC in July 2000. UPC offers undergraduate and graduate courses in the sciences, business, engineering, architecture and law, as well as degree programmes in information technology and computer science through its wholly owned subsidiary, Cibertec Institute, SA. UPC was founded in 1994 as a private, non-profit academic institution with 329 students, but grew by nearly 50 per cent per annum to about 2,500 students in 1999. This was a period of rapid growth in Peruvian private higher education, responding to the demand of parents and students who had grown weary of frequent public university closures and deterioration of learning due to frequent strikes. In 1996 a law was passed that allowed private, non-profit educational institutions to adopt any legal identity permitted for any Peruvian company. UPC chose to become a for-profit corporation to benefit from the advantages offered: (a) the university management is chosen by a board of directors rather than elected politically by faculty and has more flexibility to respond to market forces and act in the best interests of its clients – the students and their future employers; and (b) it operates more transparently as financial accounts are now audited and disclosed under the law. IFC's loan supports an investment project which expands UPC's facilities to accommodate new classrooms and laboratories and upgrade its library and computer network to support its distance education programme and provide working capital to fund the expansion of UPC's scholarship and loan programmes. UPC's managerial efficiency is reflected in the fact that the IFC loan was signed and disbursed within two months of approval.

IFC approved a US$10 million loan in August 2000 to help Universidad del Salvador expand facilities at a new campus on the outskirts of Buenos Aires, while keeping its older facilities in downtown Buenos Aires. USAL is one of the oldest and largest private universities in Argentina. The project will add about 10,000 square metres of facilities at the new campus, and permit overall enrolments to increase from 15,000 students in 1999 to about 17,000 students by 2003. The university is adding new subject offerings, such as food technology, veterinary sciences and agronomy, to its range of disciplines. The new facilities provide an improved learning environment compared to the congested conditions at its downtown location, and include a community auditorium. These are an essential part of a strategy to maintain the university's reputation as a top-quality, community-oriented learning institution, responsive to growing demand for its services. The first disbursement from the IFC loan took place in December 2000.

In November 2000 IFC approved a \$7 million loan for the Instituto Tecnológico de Buenos Aires. ITBA is the second-oldest Argentine university, has over 2,500 students and offers a variety of engineering programmes at the undergraduate and graduate levels, as well as preparatory courses and consulting services to local businesses. As in the case of USAL, this loan will support the construction of a new campus in an urban development near Buenos Aires, complementing the Institute's existing 40-year-old downtown facility located in an area which is too congested to handle future growth.

IFC approved a US\$12 million loan to Istanbul Bilgi University in Turkey in April 2001, with loan signing a month later. Bilgi's student enrolment has increased fivefold since it opened in 1995, from 914 to over 5,000 students, of which 5 per cent are graduate students. It offers undergraduate programmes in the social sciences, sciences, letters, law, communications, film, TV and music, and graduate courses in areas such as business, international relations, European Union law, and market research, among others. As with other private universities in Turkey, all instruction is in English. As required by Turkish law, the university is owned by a foundation and operates on a not-for-profit basis. It serves its urban community by providing free instruction in English, accounting and computer training. The IFC loan supports an investment project which (a) modernises and expands campus accommodation for pre-university English-language instruction as well as for the remaining university programme; (b) establishes on-line education programmes, including an e-MBA which will grow from 50 students now to 550 students by academic year 2003/04; (c) improves library and laboratory facilities; and (d) increases research and publications. The number of students enrolled by academic year 2009/10 is expected to grow to over 7,500 from the present 5,335.

A US$15 million loan was approved by IFC to Universidade do Sul de Santa Catarina (UNISUL) in Brazil in May 2001. UNISUL is a non-profit university with campuses in or near four cities in the state of Santa Catarina, offering a wide array of undergraduate subjects. Enrolments have lately grown rapidly, from 3,000 in 1990 to 19,200 ten years later. UNISUL caters heavily to a lower-middle-class clientèle, whereas Brazil's heavily subsidised public universities cater largely to upper-income groups. And UNISUL students are 53 per cent women. The IFC loan supports an investment project which expands and rehabilitates three existing campuses in order to increase enrolment by more than 10,000 students by 2006, acquires land for a new campus, updates communications and management information systems, increases faculty development, expands research facilities and a student loan programme and refinances expensive short-term debt. The project is being co-financed by the Inter-American Investment Corporation, the counterpart to IFC within the Inter-American Development Bank Group. IIC is relying on IFC's evaluation and is mirroring IFC's terms and conditions for its loan.

Finally IFC approved a US$7.5 million loan to RMIT Vietnam International University in Ho Chi Minh City, Vietnam, in June 2001. RMIT Vietnam will be the first university wholly owned and operated by RMIT (formerly the Royal Melbourne Institute of Technology) University, a public university in Melbourne, Australia. It is the first 'greenfield' university investment project supported by IFC, although the parent institution in Australia is over 100 years old. The government of Vietnam promulgated a decree in 2000 governing wholly foreign-owned, for-profit educational and medical institutions, and RMIT Vietnam is the very first company licensed under the decree. The Asian Development Bank (ADB) is co-financing the project in the same amount and on the same terms and conditions as IFC. Completion of the full campus for RMIT Vietnam could take about twelve years, at which time an enrolment of 12,000 students is expected. The IFC and ADB loans support a project which includes the first phase of construction during the period up until 2003. It will eventually be able to accommodate up to 4,150 full-time students.

Non-university specialised training centres

In May 2000 IFC approved a $230,000 loan to establish the NIIT Education and Training Centre in Accra, Ghana. The project creates a modern and fully equipped computer training school under a franchise arrangement with NIIT, Ltd of India. The franchisee is a Ghanaian trading company, Vista 2000, owned by Indian nationals with long experience in international trade in Africa and Latin America, including Nigeria and South Africa. NIIT has provided IT training to over two million students worldwide since 1982, and is the largest provider of computer education and training in India. NIIT franchises a complete training package to independent franchisees operating about 1,000 NIIT centres in India and a further 1,000 in about 30 countries in the Middle East, South-East Asia and Africa, including South Africa and Nigeria. The franchise arrangement includes management and staff training and technical supervision from the India home office. The centre's offerings include basic computer skills leading to certificates in word processing and spreadsheets, as well as Microsoft and Oracle certified professional engineering courses in networking, systems analysis and programming. NIIT also offers its own certification – the GNIIT, 'graduate of NIIT'. Enrolments are expected to grow from 456 in 2000 to over 2,500 in 2003, at full capacity. Courses introducing children to mathematics and science are also available. The IFC loan agreements were signed in January 2001.

The IFC approved a US$500,000 loan to and a 10 per cent equity stake amounting to US$80,000 in Safety Centre International, Limited (SCIL) of Port Harcourt, Nigeria, in June 2000. The project sponsor is a German engineer with extensive experience in the fire safety industry. He is well known in the Nigerian oil industry and will be the major shareholder in SCIL. SCIL is incorporated in Nigeria to train safety and fire-fighting personnel to world-class standards in the use of specialised apparatus and the maintenance of safety instruments and equipment for oil companies. SCIL's training centre will use the equipment and techniques of an industry leader in Germany. Trainees will be employees in both private and publicly owned firms. Since the closest competitors are in South Africa and Oman, SCIL will generate foreign exchange from training nationals from other countries in the region, in addition to Nigerians. The IFC loan and equity investment support a project which is building and equipping the training facility. To keep capital costs to the minimum, trainee accommodation will be purchased as needed from the nearby Port Harcourt International Airport Hotel. The project is co-financed by DEG, the German development finance agency. IFC investment documents were signed in February 2001.

Student finance

In June 2000 IFC approved a R22 million (US$3.2 million equivalent) investment in EDU-LOAN (Proprietary) Limited of South Africa (http://www.eduloan.co.za/). Black businesspeople, trade unions, financial services companies and a consortium of distance education organisations, all South African, hold major shares in EDU-LOAN. Based in Johannesburg, the company makes loans to students and working people, primarily in the public sector, for them to pursue studies, including correspondence and, increasingly, on-line courses, in currently more than 35 public and private fee-charging universities, technikons[5] and colleges/schools/training centres in South Africa, including NIIT. Working parents can also borrow from EDU-LOAN for the higher education costs of their dependants. Loans are made annually to cover tuition and related expenses for the academic year and are repayable over nine months. Loan terms include insurance against borrower death or

---

5   Technical institutes.

retrenchment. Loan repayments are made through deductions from either bank accounts or employer payrolls, limited to no more than 25 per cent of the employee's net salary. Nationwide, one-sixth of South Africa's higher education students repay through payroll deductions. The company held a portfolio of 29,000 loans after its initial two years of operation, with bad debts of just over 1 per cent of portfolio, low by worldwide industry standards. IFC's investment is in the form of (a) a R11 million loan convertible into common equity after two years, and (b) a R11 million senior loan. After IFC approved its investment the government decided to consider no further applications for deductions from the public-sector payroll, thus removing a fundamental assumption in EDU-LOAN's business model. However, the decision was reversed in February 2001 after representations were made to the Department of Treasury by South African higher education institutions which pointed to a resulting drop in student enrolments. Signing of the IFC loan documents was suspended after the government decision, and measures are being taken by the company to see whether it can sufficiently expand its portfolio of loans to private-sector employees to minimise exposure to a vulnerable feature in the business model.

In January 2001, IFC approved a partial credit risk guarantee to NIIT Limited (formerly the National Institute of Information Technology) of India for its Student Loan Programme (SLP), which Citibank-India launched in January 2000. The value of the guarantee is for the lower of 10 per cent of the programme, or Rs420 million (approximately US$9 million equivalent), over a twelve-year period. The SLP provides private financing for students participating in iGNIIT, NIIT's flagship undergraduate-level educational programme. NIIT, a listed company, is one of India's and the world's major IT training companies. As with all NIIT courses, the programme is modular, computer based and off campus. It requires three years of study, usually undertaken concurrently with pursuing an undergraduate course at a university, followed by a year of internship with stipend at one of more than 4,000 organisations. The SLP provides loans of Rs120,000 (US$2,600 equivalent), equal to 90 per cent of the cost of tuition and a computer. Loans are for a seven-year term and do not require collateral, though they require co-signing by a parent or guardian. The success of the programme depends in part on instilling disciplined, mature debt management habits among student borrowers and development of their direct relationship with the lending institution. Thus, repayment begins in the very first month after disbursement of principal, but is adjusted to the student's earning capacity. During the first three years the student pays each month only Rs1,000 to cover only 60 per cent of the interest expense on the loan, while payment of the remaining 40 per cent of the interest is capitalised and principal repayment is deferred. Then, from year four until year seven, the student makes equal monthly payments of Rs4,000 per month, equivalent to 25 to 40 per cent of expected starting salary, to pay off the loan with interest. The fixed-rate annual interest charge is 16 per cent, benchmarked in the Indian market against 21 per cent for unsecured consumer loans and 15 per cent for home mortgages. The portfolio of loans will build up over a five-year period and is expected to reach about Rs4.2 billion (approximately US$90 million), providing financing to about 25,000 additional students. While Citibank underwrites and funds the loans, IFC guarantees a third-position, sequential 10 per cent of the losses to the portfolio outstanding from borrower default. The SLP receives no government support

133

or guarantee of any kind. It is a first-of-its-kind product in the Indian consumer finance market, and as such carries significant uncertainties and risk. Citibank-India has recently conducted small pilot student loan schemes in very selected markets, but it and NIIT were unwilling to go to scale with SLP without a partial risk guarantee which IFC has provided, allowing them to multiply SLP tenfold. The IFC guarantee documents were signed in February 2001.

Issues and guideposts

Do IFC's experiences to date signify that private higher education in developing countries can provide a productive field for capital investment, whether seen from a broad public-policy or a narrower financial perspective? The short answer is that, given the youth and limited scope of the portfolio, it is obviously still too early to draw definitive conclusions. Yet it is possible briefly to discuss, at least tentatively, some of the issues that have arisen in the process of reaching investment decisions, which can become early considerations or 'guideposts' for approaching new investments more generally. Only a few among many possible issues are selected for discussion here.

Demographics and macro trends

The recent upsurge of private institutions of higher education in developing countries is strengthened by a number of broad trends and demographic factors. The large proportion of young people in much of the developing world combines with a now chronic fiscal incapacity on the part of most governments, which are facing perpetual difficulty in wresting increased tax revenues to support enough public higher education institutions of a quality good enough to meet ever-growing demand. That demand is fed by the increased integration of more countries into the global trading system, as more countries adopt export-led growth policies. Consequently, producers of goods and services are increasingly competing on quality as well as price with suppliers from distant shores, placing a premium on skills. But only a relatively few developing countries continue successfully to support high-quality public universities – Brazil's federal universities and India's Institutes of Technology and Institutes of Management come to mind, but these are few and far between and even they are progressively self-privatising by virtue of diversifying their income sources. These trends underpin the growing demand for IFC investments in higher education.

Market readiness

Private higher education institutions are more prevalent in some regions, like Latin America, and countries, like the Philippines, than in others, often for historical reasons. This prevalence has influenced the high percentage of early IFC investments in Latin America. On the other hand, in other regions, institutions in the once-dominant public ownership mode are effectively privatising themselves, making a virtue of necessity. For example, Makerere University in Uganda, a once-proud state institution, was brought virtually to its knees by desperate political and fiscal conditions in the 1970s and 1980s. But since the mid-1990s Makerere has witnessed a significant recovery by enrolling large numbers of private students, willing and able to pay for tuition, thus reducing the share of enrolment by students on state scholarships to well below half. Chronic fiscal constraint also opens the door for private student finance programmes such as EDU-LOAN in South Africa and the NIIT SLP in India, and there are signs of strong demand for investment in similar private programmes elsewhere.

Market position

A clear understanding of the local market for higher education and a strong position in it are necessary preconditions for viable capital investments. But short of insuperable barriers to entry, market competition can dislodge institutions from their clientèle. Slippage from an earlier position signals danger, and such slippage in enrolment led to cancellation of IFC's first university investment in Argentina. Careful market analysis and monitoring of changes are key aspects of the business.

Regulatory environment

As was seen in the case of EDU-LOAN, government regulations can have a major impact on the prospects for investments in higher education, as elsewhere. In many countries it is illegal for a university to be owned by a for-profit company, thus confining the private sector's participation to only a traditional, non-profit format. UPC (Peru) is a striking exception to this general rule for most of Latin America and other regions besides. If its early successes continue, it will doubtless become a model for others to emulate. Profitability above all else signifies self-sustainability. Meanwhile it is worth noting that the non-universities in the early IFC portfolio, the Computer School in Ghana, Safety Centre International, and NIIT of India, operate as for-profits.

Investor perceptions of 'bankability'

None of the universities supported by IFC had been able to obtain long-term financing from other financial institutions for their investment projects, although some had obtained short- or medium-term financing on expensive terms. IFC's overarching goal upon entering this 'frontier' investment sector has been to pioneer, i.e. to demonstrate to other institutional lenders and investors that it is possible to lend or invest in privately owned and operated education institutions and programmes in developing countries and not take losses. Indeed, it is possible to recover the loan with interest or make a reasonable return on equity.[6] This process of changing 'investor sentiment' will take time. And although interest by new private investors has been negligible thus far, a few encouraging signs of change may be appearing. For example, two regional development banks, ADB and IDB, have entered the field through co-investments with IFC. Secondly, the German development finance company DEG has co-invested with IFC in Safety Centre International and is interested in investing in EDU-LOAN. However, these institutions are government owned – as is IFC itself. Another, perhaps more telling, new sign is the decision late in 2000 by Sylvan International Universities, a

---

6   IFC (1999), *Investing in Private Education in Developing Countries*, Washington. Chapter 4 of this 'entry strategy' document, entitled 'IFC Roles in Education Investment', states:

> … *as IFC demonstrates the feasibility of profitable investment in the education sector, it can encourage other financial institutions to become active players rather than remain on the sidelines … IFC will disseminate lessons distilled from its experience to the education industry and investment community. The catalytic and knowledge roles could become IFC's most important avenues for achieving development impact.*

IFC's pioneer role is restated in a new, expanded and updated strategy paper to be published in 2001.

subsidiary of the listed and diversified American education company Sylvan Learning Systems, Inc., to acquire controlling interests in two private universities, in Chile and Mexico, with more investments expected in India and elsewhere. Sylvan's senior management had been watching IFC's earlier entry into the field. An important part of changing institutional investor perceptions will be the visibility of SIU's revenues, which already constitute over half of the parent company's revenues. Here, the typical out-year predictability of revenues flowing from admissions today should stand the sector in good stead among sceptics.

Cross-border investing

In IFC's experience, almost all sponsors are local nationals, with multinationals conspicuous by their absence thus far (relative to other industries). Of the two exceptions, the Computer School in Ghana is a case of South-South investment since the franchiser, NIIT, and the franchisee are from India. In the other exception, RMIT Vietnam, the outside investor is a state-supported university in Australia. Outside of IFC's experience, the most notable case of multinational cross-border investment in higher education is Sylvan International Universities, already mentioned.

Financial management

High standards of financial management are a *sine qua non* for sustaining increased capital inflows into private higher education in developing countries. However, this has seldom been a core strength among traditional, non-profit private universities. Where IFC becomes involved in this set of institutions, financial management transparency inevitably becomes and remains a focus of attention. Regular, externally audited financial statements are a standard requirement. This in itself can be a novelty for some institutions. A corollary is the disciplining of resource allocation decisions by financial tests and rigorous cost accounting. This may pit the reinforced strength of financial manager types against professorial defenders of deeply held beliefs regarding key curricular offerings. It may also highlight a prevailing weakness in the university subsector from a business perspective, namely 'under-trading', or the low volume of sales relative to fixed assets in the form of plant and equipment – typified in older Western universities by lush lawns and ivy-covered but often empty classroom facilities. Although the classic 'Oxbridge' or 'Ivy League' model is sometimes consciously or unconsciously the ideal facility, even for universities in low- and middle-income countries, economic and financial reality fairly often brings final plans back down to earth.

Profit versus non-profit

It would not be surprising to find that whether an institution's legal status is non-profit or for-profit has a material impact on a range of outcomes. While IFC has been investing in both types, it is only with the for-profits that investing with equity is possible. Thus far four of the investments surveyed – UPC, EDU-LOAN, NIIT, Safety Centre and RMIT Vietnam – are for-profits. Meanwhile all seven other universities – UB, UTDT, UM, USAL, ITBA, Bilgi, UNISUL – are more traditional non-profits. It will be useful to compare and contrast UPC with the other universities as the implementation of their respective investment projects unfolds in the next few years.[7] Initial impressions of UPC include the following: (a) efficient management seen in its rapid fulfilment of conditions for loan disbursement and (b) adaptability of UPC's curriculum to changing skill and qualification signals from the labour market.

Social equity

This is often a poorly understood issue in the institutional context under consideration here. And, particularly in affluent OECD nations, it is sometimes a politically overblown and easily demagogued issue. The sad truth is that in the majority of developing countries students from families in the highest income brackets very disproportionately capture public education subsidies.[8] The reasons for this inequity are by now well known. Most of the maldistribution of public education subsidies occurs in higher education, with somewhat less at the secondary level. This is because the poor have already largely dropped off the school 'ladder' – that is, assuming they even entered primary school to begin with – long before they can enjoy the larger public subsidies which are concentrated at the secondary and especially higher levels of the ladder.[9] Thus the obvious first step in tackling

7   The circumstances surrounding the creation of RMIT Vietnam – a very new greenfield project, ownership by a foreign state university, operating under a still-untested decree promulgated by a socialist government – are sufficiently extraordinary to give pause in interpreting the meaning of the rubric 'for profit' in this case, and, thus, in generalising lessons from its forthcoming experience.

8   World Bank (2000), *World Development Report 2000/1*, Washington, table 5.1 and paragraphs 5.28–5.29.

9   The most common reasons for dropout in the developing world context are also frequently misunderstood. While school fees and other monetised costs receive most attention, by far the largest economic barrier is not financial cost but

the problem of limited representation by the poor in either public or private higher education is to prevent or at least reduce early dropout in the primary and then the secondary grades. Nonetheless, virtually all the private higher education institutions that approach IFC for support attempt to offer their own helping hand to the relatively few poor who manage to seek admission, either through scholarships or through student loan schemes.

Student finance

None of the private higher education institutions surveyed receives any government or other subsidies.[10] By the same token, all of them depend either very heavily or exclusively on student fees for their income. But since they all operate in low- or middle-income countries, they obviously contend with some price resistance on the part of at least a portion of their potential markets. Almost all private universities provide some scholarship funds, often including a financial need as well as an academic merit criterion in making awards. But scholarship funds – however financed – are intrinsically in limited supply. The logical solution for large-scale student support is student finance, usually loans to students or their parents. This is an area of potentially prime strategic

---

'opportunity cost' on account of the large amounts of time absorbed by schooling, day in and day out. Time is a highly prized resource, especially for the poor, since time is required even by young children to help provide daily food and shelter for oneself and one's closest kin in a subsistence-level household. Schooling competes for large portions of this time and often loses out to the basic necessities. Reducing fees does not address the crux of the problem.

10 Bilgi University is entitled to apply for a small subsidy from the Turkish government, but how much it would actually receive depends year to year and quarter to quarter on the severity of the government's fiscal constraint. It prudently chooses not to apply.

importance to the broad expansion of private higher education in developing countries. One lesson already learned by IFC is the high failure rate when universities attempt to manage student lending on their own, as though they could will themselves into banks. The repeated result is that such well-intentioned but flawed efforts woefully underestimate the skills and culture required by professional credit institutions, and ultimately produce a stack of bad debts to burden the university's balance sheet. This outcome creates opportunities for financial institutions in developing countries to offer consumer products to help families invest in developing the human capital of their members. Banks with the interest and skills in consumer credit, like Citibank in India, should be aggressively seeking to build relationships with their likely best future customers by offering student or parent loans. And insurance companies, such as those in the Philippines,[11] have the opportunity to sell annuitised college savings plans to families with young children who dream of going to university one day. Paid-up savings plans could also be used as collateral for reduced interest rates on student loans.

---

11   IFC (1999), *Investment Opportunities in Private Education in Developing Countries*, Washington, case study 3, by Jocelyn I. Bolante, President, Prudential Life Plan, Inc., the Philippines.

7 WHO SHOULD PAY FOR HE?

David Halpern

Introduction: The political and ideological context

The funding and structures of Britain's universities need reform. The current arrangements are an uncomfortable compromise born of the political timidity of recent governments and the institutional rigidity of the universities themselves.

When the current government was swept to power in 1997, Higher Education (HE) was an issue it did not really want to touch. Even a cursory analysis of the then existing funding arrangements indicated that, in terms of social justice, reform was badly needed. Through general taxation, the whole community was funding the further advancement of the most able and advantaged minority – it was clearly regressive. This was even more striking in a context in which the more vocationally oriented courses favoured by the less advantaged often had to be paid for by the individuals taking them. Yet at the same time, the new administration was genuinely terrified that reform of HE funding would trigger a massive middle-class revolt. The hard-won support of middle England – including the professionals who had once so firmly supported the Conservatives – would be up in arms at the loss of one of their most prized privileges.

So the administration initially sat tight. It was greatly aided in this simple plan by the fact that it was the previous administration which had started a process of funding reform and, perhaps even more so, by the lumbering and divided deliberations of the HE sector itself, notably manifested through the Dearing inquiry. Even so, the truth is that the government thought that it was going to have a much harder time over HE – and especially over the introduction of fees – than it did. A few lectures were cancelled in days of protest (only to be rescheduled so as not to inconvenience students). There were some student protests – but perhaps not more than at any other time. But most importantly, there weren't really any *parent* protests.

But something very important has happened. Five years ago, many considered that there was a self-evident principle that 'education should be free'. Even three years ago, a very active on-line discussion organised by the e-based think tank Nexus showed that university lecturers still felt very strongly that a university education should be free as a matter of principle.[1] When the THES reported the Nexus debate on its front page under the headline 'Nexus proposes private Oxbridge', it still caused quite a storm.[2] But now that fees have been in place for a few years, and people are still voting Labour, one can expect that the next round of discussion and reform will have a very different feel. In the Labour government's second term, we shall see a far more mature and self-confident approach to reform that will be more at ease with the full range of possibilities for HE.

---

1 See Halpern (1997), 'What's your degree worth to you?', *New Statesman*, 19 December 1997, pp. 22–4, for a report on the debate. Nexus has now been reformed into Policybrief.org, an e-based information service for UK think tanks.

2 *Times Higher Education Supplement*, 21 November 1997.

A simple principle to guide reform – who benefits pays

Let us first deal with the claim that social justice demands that we have good free education for all. It works well as a principle at primary and secondary levels, where education is a universal experience and an important precondition of opportunity for all. But the experience of university is very different. It is an opportunity for a subset of the population – the talented and advantaged – to help extend and fulfil their true potential. If free it would represent a gross redistribution of resources from the poor and disadvantaged to the affluent and able. Furthermore, an eighteen-year-old can be asked to take some responsibility for his or her life choices in a way that a five-year-old cannot.

The simple alternative is that we require those who benefit from HE to fund it. This principle proves a powerful guide to the reform of HE. As we shall see, it is a mistake to assume that it will lead to adoption of the US-style private university model.

Using the principle, we can argue that in so far as graduates receive substantial personal benefits from higher education in the form of higher future earnings, they should be expected to contribute to the cost of that education. Interestingly, this argument was employed by David Blunkett in the debate about the introduction of fees. Estimates of the scale of this personal benefit vary. Sceptical views of the scale of the benefit are expressed through the 'credentialism literature' – that the higher earnings of graduates simply express their underlying abilities rather than any value-added quality provided by the university education itself. However, after three decades of argument on this point there now seems fairly widespread agreement that there is a real financial payoff to individuals in participating in HE – perhaps averaging a 25 per cent increase in lifetime earnings. Given this, there appears to be a very strong case for passing on at least some of the costs of HE to those students who pass through it.

But this is only the start of the argument. The principle makes the case not just for fees, but for fees differentiated by likely returns in the market. Several other questions follow. Should the 'fees' for HE be flat across institutions and subjects, or should they vary? Is there a counter-argument that HE should be subsidised? And how should such fees be levied?

State subsidies and the issue of differential fees

Despite arguing that fees in HE were justified by higher graduate earnings, David Blunkett stuck with the idea of equal fees for all. This makes little sense. A student who goes to Oxford or Cambridge can expect to earn considerably more than one at another university. Similarly, a student studying a subject like law or management can expect to earn far more than one studying social sciences or social work. By the 'who benefits pays' principle, these differential future earnings imply differential fees. Oxbridge students should pay more because they will earn more.

But not all the benefits of higher education flow to individual graduates, and this is where the argument becomes more complex.[3] First, some of the benefits that flow from a more educated population are felt by the whole community. For example, the fact that someone has a particular skill can improve the productivity of others. In other words, education generally has positive externalities – individuals' efforts to educate themselves also tend to benefit those around them. Second, there are some disciplines –

3   See, for example, the work of Professor John Bynner at the Institute of Education.

medicine being the obvious example – where the true cost of the training is expensive relative to eventual salaries, but where the activity and knowledge are seen as being of great value to the community. In such cases, the community either has to be prepared to subsidise the training or to pay higher salaries. Third, at least some of the activities of universities – notably research – benefit the whole community rather than any particular individual. This is especially true of 'cutting edge' or pure research which no individual company would ever fund. In all these respects, the argument 'who benefits pays' leads to the conclusion that at least some form of public subsidy for universities should continue, albeit a more discriminating one than we have at present.

It is this 'line in the sand', between private gain and public advantage, that the universities and DfEF should be working hard to establish. An obvious building block here is the distinction as already made between the HEFCE teaching grant and the HEFCE research grant. The former, in so far as it results in private gain, might be significantly reduced or eliminated, but the latter, in so far as it represents a public good, should perhaps be substantially increased.[4] Without this line in the sand, or the accounts, there will be no coherent case against the Treasury's on-going demands to edge up student fees and progressively eliminate public subsidy.

If the HEFCE teaching grant were phased out, this would currently lead to a shortfall of about £4,600 per student per year in most universities, and around £7,100 per student per year at Oxbridge – and potentially substantially more in some subjects. What we need to do is to calculate, as best we can, the value of the

---

4   There is an important side issue here about whether the HEFCE grant is really the best way to fund research. A case can be made that this is much better done – in the sense of producing better research – through the research councils.

positive externalities of HE. The calculation is made somewhat more difficult by the fact that some of the positive externalities of HE may be as much social as directly economic, such as in the form of increased social tolerance or civic mindedness. Nonetheless, we need to attempt this calculation in order to obtain a figure for the appropriate scale of public subsidy to reduce the fees paid by individual students, noting that it could vary significantly across subjects.

How should 'fees' be paid?

Once we have decided that there is a strong case for individual students to fund their own education, at least partly, the thorny issue arises of the form in which these fees should be paid. It is arguable that the worst of all worlds is to have fees payable up front. Even the private universities in the USA work hard to avoid this situation, given that it can put off students from less affluent backgrounds.

In fact, the UK already has a well-documented example of the dangers of an up-front deregulated fee system. In the early 1990s, university-based training for those embarking on a career in the legal professions was reformed. The Legal Practice Course – the one-year vocational training required as a prerequisite for entry into the legal professions – was deregulated. This was a course for which universities charged fees, and for which grants were not normally paid. At the same time, there was a massive increase in the number of students doing Common Professional Examination (CPE), the conversion course for students wishing to switch to law after completing a degree in another subject. Understandably, cash-strapped universities happily increased the number of places on these courses. The combined effect of these changes was simultaneously to increase the cost of legal training while also generating an oversupply of trainee lawyers. This meant not only that many students faced the prospect of £10,000 or more in costs in order to have the chance of entering the professions, but that the probability of finding a job as a lawyer also fell. The latter meant many students could not even obtain loans. The net result was that students doing the CPE, despite being concentrated in the new universities, developed a class profile more skewed towards the affluent than any other student group in the country – even more so than Oxbridge itself. [5] In short, up-front fees – and especially when numbers are unregulated – can be a disaster for the social-class profile of the intake. This example should also serve as a warning to those who would consider following the recent Australian model of using the levels of university fees to regulate sections of the labour market.

There are various ways around this type of fee-created problem, many of which can be seen in the élite universities of the US and elsewhere. The first is to offer scholarships – or to have 'needs blind' admissions, where students are first admitted on the basis of ability, then the fees set according to their ability to pay. This is effectively a form of means testing, with the affluent charged at a higher rate to subsidise the cost of scholarships. Data supplied by David Robertson (Liverpool University) and David Donald (Glasgow University) suggest that this system can work respectably well. They reported in the Nexus debate that despite Harvard charging around $23,000 per annum for tuition fees,

---

5   See Halpern (1994), 'Entry into the legal professions: the law student cohort study years 1 and 2', The Law Society, London.

ethnic minorities were at least as well represented as at Oxbridge (perhaps not a great claim), and around two-thirds of the intake were from 'public', as opposed to private, schools.

Nonetheless, there are serious downsides to an exclusive reliance on a scholarship or means-tested system. Less confident applicants, disproportionately from less privileged backgrounds, may be put off by the huge number of forms probing background information. There will be some inevitable injustices; and, as Rupert Wilkinson (Sussex University) – an expert on the financing of US universities – pointed out in the debate, in practice many universities will seek to direct extra funds to financing merit- rather than need-based scholarships, and these again tend to favour the already advantaged.

The second, increasingly familiar alternative is to offer loans repayable after graduation. One important practical issue, especially if the use of loans becomes extensive, is whether they are available to all and at the same rates. Great caution has to be used when private lenders are involved, especially as regards cherry-picking the wealthy over the less secure and offering them lower rates. One option for Oxford and Cambridge, though probably not elsewhere, suggested by Stewart Wood at Oxford, would be for wealthy universities to use their assets to underwrite a loan system based on need.

Of course, it is repaying the loan, rather than the granting of it, which concerns most students! Some comfort is gained from making repayment income contingent – payment is deferred until the individual starts earning money in the labour market. A more fundamental issue is that, beyond crude deferral, loan repayment tends to be insensitive to eventual earnings. The woman who takes career breaks will pay just as much as a colleague who does not; the lawyer who specialises in family law pays as much as his colleague who works in the City on commercial property and earns ten times more.

A further potential injustice pointed out by Stuart White, previously professor at the Massachusetts Institute of Technology (MIT) in the USA but now back at Oxford, is that a rapid movement towards fees has the makings of a huge generational injustice. Today's students will be expected to pay a much higher proportion of the cost of their education than those of even a few years ago, while those who graduated in the past and are currently earning good salaries – partly as a result of their university education – paid little or nothing. This logically suggests that we should be looking not only to student fees but to past graduate taxes too – a 'windfall' graduate tax though politically this would not be attractive.

The potential injustices of loans direct us toward a simple alternative – a tax paid on earnings. This appears to lead us back to where we started from – HE funded out of conventional income tax! But there is an important difference. What we are trying to do here is to fairly apportion the costs of HE to the benefits captured by private individuals, linking the 'right' or availability of an expensive university education with the 'responsibility' for its cost. If we just use general income tax, then we lose this important linkage. The semi-skilled worker who did not go to university and who puts in 60 hours a week to bring home the same wage as a part-time graduate is contributing as much to the cost of HE – a basic injustice. A much fairer variant on the loan or general income tax model would be for graduates to pay a small surcharge on their future incomes – perhaps 2 per cent extra for fifteen years after graduation. This graduate tax – hypothecated directly back to the universities – would establish a clear link between the cost and benefit of HE to individuals but without the problems and injustices of up-front fees or income-insensitive loans.

Capital grants: a radical alternative?

If you do not like the conclusion that we should fund HE from a graduate tax, there is a radical alternative that would share most of its advantages. We could decide, as a society, to issue every eighteen-year-old with an individual capital grant sufficient to cover the cost of going to university – but not require him or her to use the money in this way.

The idea of universal capital grants has been proposed by various figures as a way of addressing the problem of widening capital inequalities. For example, Ackerman proposed a grant of $80,000 in the USA, Le Grand and Hutton proposed a grant of £10,000, and, most recently, the Institute for Public Policy Research proposed a baby bond of £1,000 to be given to every child and invested in trust until the child reached eighteen. In all cases, the authors suggest that the capital grant come with some restrictions as to how it may be spent so that it doesn't just get 'blown' on drugs, fast cars or the holiday of a lifetime. Typically, suggested permitted uses include starting up a business, funding education, a contribution to a pension scheme and, sometimes, the down payment on a first house.

Even two years ago, this idea appeared completely fanciful, and was not even on the very edge of the political radar. It still is completely off the radar in the USA, but in the UK the idea is now receiving serious consideration – at least in the form of the low-cost 'baby bond'. I have always much liked the idea of capital grants, and would suggest that the universities should too. Indeed, one might propose that the universities should be lobbying strongly for an ambitious form of capital grant. For these grants – as well as having extremely desirable social justice properties – offer the universities their best shot at the kind of freedom they have come to long for. A system of capital endowments fundamentally shifts power away from the government as the purchaser of HE services to the individual prospective student. At the same time, presuming a reasonable level of grant, it creates something akin to a level financial playing field for those prospective students.

Who else has a stake in our universities?

Students are not the only beneficiaries of HE. As already mentioned, much of the activity of universities has a public-good dimension – especially research. In so far as this is the case, HE merits proportionate public grants. But there are also other categories of beneficiaries.

It is increasingly appreciated that universities create benefits for the regions in which they are embedded. The classic UK example of this is the 'Cambridge phenomenon', whereby large numbers of high-tech industries have become established in science parks around the university, feeding off and in turn reinforcing the intellectual capital of the university. Prudent local and regional authorities seek to reinforce and maximise these local benefits, in effect creating a new funding stream for the universities. The question arises as to whether sufficient sums of these local financial benefits return to the universities. The answer is probably not. Indeed, the success of the local region can sometimes throw up considerable costs for the university concerned, such as in higher house prices and competition for staff. Furthermore, unlike firms, universities generally never consider relocating, putting them in a weak position as regards bargaining for their share of the joint local benefit.

On this point, it is instructive to consider what the local and regional reaction would be to the announcement by a university – or a large section of it – of a move somewhere else in the country, or even overseas. How much would – or should – we pay to keep Oxford's biotechnology, Cambridge's physics or LSE's social sciences from relocating to California? Even the most basic back-of-an-envelope calculations suggest local regions gain a great deal from the presence of HE, and rational funding should in some way reflect this, such as in sponsorship from local industry or support from the local tax base.

Another interesting stakeholding group in a university is its past graduates. In so far as the value of a degree rests on the status of the institution that bestowed it, past graduates have a vested interest in maintaining that status. It would be far too cynical to suggest that this is the only reason behind the huge generosity of the alumni of the élite universities of as Harvard in the USA and Oxbridge in the UK, but it certainly helps. If we are serious about the idea of creating a learning society, then higher education should not simply end with graduation. The universities should legitimately reorientate themselves to their past graduates and ask what they can do that will be of continuing value to them, be that refresher courses, research or access to facilities. If a 'graduate tax' as mentioned above were enacted, perhaps to help fund the scheme of capital endowments, graduates would effectively be asked to fund their old universities. Under such circumstances, they will surely ask what the universities are doing for them in return. The occasional good reference will not be enough.

Should universities be privatised?

There is no necessary relationship between the charging of fees and going private. State-funded or -run bodies can charge fees. For example, you have to pay to get a passport. Similarly, private institutions can be state funded such that they are free at the point of provision, such as the health services of many industrialised nations. The real question is therefore one about 'what works?' In particular, it is appropriate to ask whether the institutional structure delivers value, broadly conceived, and whether it is responsive and accountable to its stakeholders.

The discussion above concerning funding illustrates that there are a number of parties who have a stake in what the universities do apart from those who teach in them. It is unreasonable to ask government, students, past graduates and others to fund the universities and then give them no say in their organisation.

One option would be that the organisation of universities should resemble that of a true stakeholding structure, with major decisions made by boards that include representatives of the state, current students and past graduates, as well as university personnel. Such a mechanism might be favoured by a government concerned not to see the cost of a university education in the UK leap upwards at a spectacular rate as academics – not entirely unreasonably – awarded themselves substantial catch-up salaries. However, the thought of such decision-making boards surely sends shudders down the spine. The crude mirroring of stakeholders in a decision-making body is not necessary as long as those stakeholders have other ways of effectively expressing their interests to the organisation, including sanctioning it when those interests are ignored. This, of course, is something that markets can sometimes do very effectively.

Once prospective students are paying fees, a market comes into play – provided a reasonable level of information exists – that will reward the best and punish the worst institutions and departments. As long as basic social justice requirements are met, such as ensuring that all students have the means to attend any particular course, the state should not need to govern the universities further. In this context, the state might wish to have in place some regulation over differences in fees between institutions to ensure that some élite institutions did not simply elect to raise fees tenfold and educate only the extremely wealthy. But there would seem to be no reason why the state should continue to control salaries or detail the content or form of HE teaching.

On the other hand, it seems perfectly reasonable that the state should wish to exercise continued influence over the overall patterning and level of publicly funded research, though this can be done perfectly adequately through research councils and the like. Similarly, there might be a strong case for ensuring that past graduates should have a say over the form of the provision of services that universities offer to their graduates, from the supplying of references to lifelong learning events.

But having 'a say' should not mean determining. It is increasingly common for funding to be offered in the form of a matched spending offer. In other words, 'we'll put in X to fund the Y that we're interested in, if you match it'. Such funding with strings, if used excessively, soaks up the institution's discretionary cash and with it its ability to innovate or offer a valuable contribution to the future agenda.

Reform beyond funding

There are many important issues in HE beyond the question of funding. In fact, one of the major problems in debates about funding is that they distract us from many other issues on which we should be focusing. This issue is endemic to institutional arrangements that have little correspondence between their funding base and their users – the organisation inevitably ends up spending too much time focusing on the funder at the expense of the user. Just to ensure that this paper does not entirely fall into that same trap, let us consider three such issues.

All institutions accrue vested interests that may unhelpfully distort their structure, and we can safely assume that the same is true of universities. We should be open to the idea of takeovers inside the HE sector, such that some more successful universities might take over the management of others. Apart from offering the possibility of substantial cost savings, such takeovers should keep our VCs and senior figures on their toes to guard against complacency. Similarly, while the Quality Assurance Agency (QAA) increasingly looks like a bizarre import from Stalinist Russia, it is important that universities deliver useful information to inform the choices of prospective students, and this is likely to require some forms of standardised comparison. My own view is that I would rather trust a standardised survey of university students themselves than the clumsy bureaucratic inspections of occasional outsiders. But at the same time, I recognise that some external regulation is likely to be necessary to get information flowing in a trustworthy form.

A consideration of reform in the UK context cannot be considered complete without considering the Oxbridge question. These are exceptional institutions with remarkable international reputations, and this fact should make reformers tread carefully. This said, it would be quite wrong to think that Oxbridge is not in need of reform. In terms of differential funding and therefore fees, as long as there is good reason to think that Oxbridge does provide added value over other institutions, then such differential fees are perfectly justified. However, the wrangle over the Oxbridge fee last time around, much to the confusion of outsiders, was not really about this, but more about a power struggle between college and university. In this context, it is legitimate to ask what makes us confident that such wrangles are correctly resolved – in terms of educational or research value – and whether Oxbridge has the institutional mechanisms to reform itself and evolve effectively. My personal view is that Oxbridge, like so many large organisations, does not have such mechanisms and will need help to establish them.

To take just one example, the Oxbridge colleges continue to be based on a model of scholarship from about two hundred or more years ago, when virtually all scholars were either theological or intellectually curious generalists. The intellectual organisation of colleges as almost entirely non-specialist derives from this period – in other words, virtually all colleges offer all subjects. The contemporary intellectual justification for this arrangement, familiar to all Oxbridge dons, is that some of the most interesting intellectual exchanges and possibilities come from people from very different subjects seeing connections across the intellectual divide. Hence, the young literary scholar at dinner, after a conversation with the resident physicist, might discover that quantum mechanics actually describes the problems of modern literature; or the organic chemist suddenly sees in the ramblings of the economist opposite the structure of a molecule that had previously escaped him. In support of this position is the finding from historians of science that major breakthroughs have often occurred at the hands of disciplinary outsiders.

But the problem with this analysis is that while interesting and innovative ideas can arise when people from different disciplines come together, this can only be the case when these people also have enough in common still to have an overlapping language and interest. Despite the Research Assessment Exercise (RAE), economists and sociologists really can benefit from talking to one another, as can chemists and physicists, historians and classicists, and so on. But if you stretch the boundaries too far, the only thing that such scholars have got left to talk about together is what colour to paint the library, how bad the food is, or what to plant in the garden next year. Yet it is almost unimaginable that Oxbridge and its colleges could embark on a systematic review or reform that would lead to more rational clustering of subjects within colleges. The point is not to specify here to what degree such reform *should* occur, but to illustrate that the institution seems incapable of even beginning to embark on it.

A final issue for brief consideration is the tension in universities between teaching, research and administration. It seems odd that we promote people on the basis of their research and then make it impossible for them to do any. Perhaps this is partly a variant on the old question of why Britain is so good at inventing things, and so bad at exploiting them. I shall not attempt to answer the question here, but simply wish to flag it up as a continuing puzzle and matter of concern.

An illuminating case study of the extent of this problem is unfolding in the form of the much-heralded Cambridge–MIT (CMI) link, proudly announced by Gordon Brown last year. But the CMI project is struggling to find its way, precisely because the whole culture of the British end of the link is so far removed from the American style. Manufacturing problems are not routinely viewed as intellectual problems by us, nor do we instinctively consider the bottom line or application of our work. It may be that part of this curious disconnection and disinterest is born of our universities' long history of passive dependence on the public purse, and that the kinds of changes discussed above will bring with them new ways of thinking in the intellectual as well as the managerial domain. Even more important may be our attitude towards administration and administrators. Effective American universities have within them well-paid, highly able and effective administrators. We, in contrast, look down on administration, begrudgingly employ a few secretaries, and then load our professors onto endless committees. If we want to get universities doing more quality research, then we had better figure out how to get individual academics doing more quality research, and that will probably mean the creation of a new generation of specialist skilled administrators.

Conclusion: tomorrow's university

Further reform of the funding and regulation of Britain's universities is to be expected in the near future. The political wariness that characterised the Labour government's approach to the issue in its first term will be replaced by a much more confident and potentially radical approach in the second.

This paper has argued that a 'who benefits pays' principle is a useful guide to funding reform. Taking all things into account, it seems that the universities should move towards funding based on at least four sources. First, future students should be required to contribute a substantial proportion of the costs of their higher education. These fees should vary between institutions and courses, not only because of varying costs, but also as a reflection of varying impacts on lifetime earnings. In so far as fees are justified by increased future earnings, a hypothecated 'graduate tax' – a small supplement on income tax in the fifteen years after graduation – would be a fairer repayment method than income-contingent loans. A radical alternative would be up-front fees twinned with the introduction of capital grants for all at eighteen. The grants would be sufficient to cover the individual's contribution to university fees, but could also be applied to alternative uses by those who choose not to attend university, such as starting up a business.

Second, the universities should receive grants from government in so far as their work contributes to the public good. These would cover much of the cost of research and could also include subsidies for subjects rated of high public value in which the real cost of training was high in comparison to market rewards (for example, medicine). A more general partial subsidy can also be justified on the basis that HE generates positive social and economic externalities not captured by individual graduates, but the scale of this has yet to be accurately calculated.

Third, additional revenue would be raised from past graduates, possibly initially part-funding the system of capital grants. At the same time, the universities should look to deepen their relationships with past graduates, not least to make lifetime learning into more of a reality. Finally, industry would continue to fund specific projects of direct value to them, as occurs now, and local and regional authorities should be asked to make some contribution to universities in their area in so far as the local economy directly benefits from their presence.

The introduction of fees does not require that universities become fully privately funded, though some might wish to adopt this form. The argument here suggests that universities might better adopt the form of mutuals, reflecting their complex mix of stakeholder interests. A central objective, however, is that funding and any corresponding reform should achieve an HE sector able to innovate, and orientated to the needs and interests of students, rather than to the deadening hand of government bureaucracy.

Finally, it was noted that there are a number of important and interesting issues that lie beyond the perennial arguments over funding. These include the systematic feedback of information from students and graduates to prospective students; the need for Oxbridge to reform itself; and encouraging a more entrepreneurial and applied culture within HE.

The coming century is one in which the role of universities will become more significant. It is to be hoped that, in order to take advantage of this opportunity, those within HE will lead the next round of reform rather than be reluctant partners within it.

8 THE GREAT HIGHER EDUCATION INVESTMENT SWINDLE[1]

Duke Maskell

> Society benefits from higher education to the extent that a
> graduate pays higher taxes, as well as earning a greater
> amount post-tax … Thirdly, graduates may enhance the
> productivity of other people in ways not captured in their
> own incomes (one aspect of so-called externalities).
>
> National Committee of Inquiry into Higher Education
> (1997), Annexe C, para. 19

Last year, in his February 2000 Greenwich speech, David Blunkett called for 'a rigorous debate on university funding'. Baroness Blackstone added that the government was going to look at 'all the options'. But Mr Blunkett and the Baroness are deceiving someone – if not us, themselves. For there is one option the government has no intention of debating, rigorously or otherwise: that of making massive cuts in university funding by making massive cuts in the number of university places.

The government won't – can't – debate that option because of its fixed belief that the £6 billion of taxes spent each year on the universities isn't spent but invested. It's prudent, it's necessary, it's profitable. It returns to us, over time, forty-fold. And why does the

---

1   This chapter is based on the first chapter of Duke Marshall and Ian Robinson, *The New Idea of a University*, Haven Books, Burbage House, 83 Curtain Road, London EC2A 3BS.

government, and just about everybody else in British politics, left, right and centre, believe this so strongly?

Because they all say it so often.

And yet, not so very long ago, the government welcomed a report which showed perfectly clearly that the arguments for believing in universities as investments are about as strong as those for alien abduction. There's no proof that aliens don't abduct people, and there's no proof that the universities aren't an investment. Otherwise neither case has much going for it. That, at least, is what it says in the Dearing Report.[2] And the Dearing Report so impressed the present government that it rewarded its chairman with a peerage; and then announced that it was going to increase the percentage of people going to university from one in three to one in two, because it was such a great investment.

Which I think must mean that no one in the government has read the relevant parts of the report. But that isn't perhaps so very surprising, because I don't think Lord Dearing can have read them very carefully either. He has learned from them that higher education can be a very good thing but not precisely who it can, and can't, be a good thing for. The individual, subsidised student, he knows, can make it a good thing for himself: we must 'encourage the student to see him/herself as an investor in receipt of a service, and to seek, as an investor, value for money and a good return from the investment' (ch. 22, para. 19). But whether or not the taxpayer can do the same is something he can't make up his mind about. He calls the £6 billion of taxes that go into higher education every year both an 'investment', with a 'backlog' which needs to be

2   National Committee of Inquiry into Higher Education (1997), *Higher Education in the Learning Society* (the 'Dearing Report'), HMSO, London.

'addressed', and 'costs', 'expenditure', 'funding', in which he looks forward to the government's 'delivering' a reduction.

The sub-reports in Dearing

The parts of his report he ought to have paid more attention to are two sub-reports by professional economists, which, between them, do make it clear what returns, on average, individual graduates and taxpayers each get: number seven, by Colin Sausman and James Steel of the Department of Education and Employment, on the 'Contribution of graduates to the economy: rates of return', and number eight, by Professor Norman Gemmell of the Department of Economics, University of Nottingham, on 'Externalities to higher education: a review of the new growth literature'.[3] These have the authority of the best economic judgement (in the government's judgement) the government could buy. Whatever economic case these two reports make out for past and future expansion of university education is the official economic case for it. What other case could there be?

These two reports ought to be well known, by everyone who pays taxes – especially those who haven't got degrees or who, having got them from the University of Buckingham, have paid the full cost themselves.

For the graduates whose university education is subsidised from taxes, their education has proved a good investment; and its value as investment is easily understood. The student's investment is what he loses in (net) earnings during the period of study (and,

---

3   Both are contained in National Committee of Inquiry into Higher Education, op. cit. All references that follow are to this report.

now, what he pays in fees) and his return is the higher net wages he can expect to earn over a working lifetime as a graduate. This is what the economists call the 'private rate of return'. If the graduate's costs are low enough, for instance because of generous subsidy by the state from taxes, and if the higher earnings are high enough, for instance in part because some jobs are reserved for graduates, it makes sound financial sense to get a degree. According to Sausman and Steel, the average yield has probably been about 12.5 per cent a year (their Table 2.2). (But that figure is based on ten-year-old data and doesn't take into account the fact that maintenance grants have been replaced by tuition charges.)

But the financial benefit their subsidised education confers on those with degrees supplies in itself no clue as to whether or not a large higher education system sustained by subsidies makes good economic sense either for non-graduates or for the economy as a whole. Do non-graduates benefit economically from subsidising the education of graduates? If they don't, where is the justice of the subsidy, and where is the political case for continuing to expand higher education through the tax system? If they don't, can there even be any economic case for the expansion? Professor Gemmell says:

> If the gains from HE (in the form of higher wages) are all
> reaped by graduates themselves there is no immediate
> economic case for subsidising the HE system. State-funded
> education would merely be taxing some individuals (with
> resulting efficiency losses) in order to enhance the private
> gains to others. Indeed the subsidy will encourage some
> individuals at the margin to undertake a socially wasteful
> investment. (1.3)

So, the official (but unpublicised) view seems to be that if it were only the graduates themselves who benefited from their subsidised education it would be both unjust and bad for the economy. Well, is it?

On the (doubtful) assumptions (see later) that graduates are more productive than non-graduates, that it is their education that makes them so and that their greater productivity is measured by their higher pay, Sausman and Steel are able to calculate the 'standard social rate of return' – the economic benefit society as a whole gets from graduates, which is analogous to the 'private rate' which the graduates themselves get. The method of calculation is the same as that for the 'private rate' but the measures are somewhat different, and the results are more problematic because some of the costs and benefits cannot be measured directly but have to be inferred from proxies. The costs are the full cost of tuition and the GDP lost to the economy as measured by the students' forgone earnings. The benefit is the supposed higher productivity of graduates as measured by the greater cost of employing them, that is, higher gross wages plus employers' higher national insurance and pension contributions. The 'standard social rate of return' accounts for the first two ways in which Lord Dearing says that graduates benefit society as a whole, by earning more after tax and paying more tax.

But economists also (sometimes) suppose that graduates are not only more productive themselves but make the non-graduates around them, both in their own and other firms, more productive too: in the phraseology of economics, there are beneficial 'externalities' or 'spillovers' to higher education, what a non-economist might think of as 'crumbs' (as in 'from a rich man's table'). Professor Gemmell continues:

If higher education does render educated individuals more

productive, the case for subsidising them rests on there being beneficial spillovers (externalities) to others. There may be spillovers both within and between firms so that gains to the economy as a whole exceed those accruing to the educated individuals. (1.4)

This is Dearing's third way. These three ways in which graduates are supposed to benefit the economy need looking at more closely. Numbered headings might be helpful.

Beneficial spillovers?

I: Ways 1 and 2: earning more after tax and paying higher taxes – the 'standard social rate of return'

From the end figures of Sausman's and Steel's calculations, it might sound to a non-economist as if all those without subsidised degrees do quite well from their compulsory tax investment in the education of people with them, for they share a return on the investment, apparently, of about 8 per cent (Table 2.1) which, though less than the 12.5 per cent the graduates themselves get, still sounds pretty good. But what non-economists are unlikely to guess is that the non-graduates don't actually, themselves, *get* any of this social benefit. 'Society' gets it, but through its graduate representatives only. Whether higher wages do measure higher productivity is a question to be returned to below but, whether or not they do, it is surely startling to realise (startling for laymen, I mean) that, if we are looking for the economic benefits to non-graduates, it would make no difference at all to the so-called standard social rate of return calculation if, as Professor Gemmell suggests is possible, 'the gains from HE [were] all reaped by the graduates themselves' (1.3). Even if the non-graduates got not a sniff of any benefits going, by way of taxation or otherwise, they would still be reckoned, according to the – what shall we call them? – counterintuitive accounting procedures used by economists, to enjoy 'a standard social rate of return' on their subsidy of other people's education of 8 per cent. It's as if someone else could enjoy benefits on your behalf!

It would equally make no difference to the social rate of return, of course, if the Chancellor (like the Sultan in the following story) took all the graduates' higher earnings in tax. It would still make no difference if he handed it over to the non-graduates straightaway.

The economist father of a friend of my son's explained the point to me. 'The distribution of the benefits,' he said, 'has nothing to do with economics. The "distribution problem" belongs in ethics.' He illustrated the point. 'Suppose,' he said, 'there was a very poor country which, because oil was discovered there, became, in a very short time, immensely rich; but all the riches were taken by the Sultan for himself; and not only that, but the Sultan, being a cruel and tyrannical man, used his new riches to increase his own power and to rob and oppress his subjects, making everyone but himself even poorer and more wretched than they had been before. Now is that country, as a whole, richer or poorer than before? In the eyes of us economists, the country as a whole, all its increased poverty and wretchedness notwithstanding, is immensely richer and has come to enjoy a marvellously high "social rate of return" on its oil investment. After all, we mustn't forget that the Sultan himself belongs to the country (even if it does seem rather as if it's the country that belongs to him). All we economists are interested in is total GDP. Everything after that is "the distribution problem". Nothing to do with us, old chap. You want someone in ethics, down the road.'

Even if the greater productivity of graduates were proven, the 'standard social return' would not, then, in itself justify any subsidies to higher education. It does not – as it seems to – answer the question whether it is just or not for non-graduates to subsidise the education of graduates; and it does not – as it seems to – answer the question whether or not those subsidies benefit the economy as a whole. The economic question is whether public subsidy is more efficient than a free market in which all the investment comes from the graduate. Nobody much discusses this. The economic case for subsidy must then depend upon:

II: The third way – 'externalities' or 'crumbs'

A. The theory

First of all, are there any economic theories that posit the existence of crumbs? Well, unfortunately, Professor Gemmell says, 'Traditional human capital theory has ... little to say about externalities', 'neo-classical growth theory [provides] no scope for externalities' and 'traditional growth theory [gives] no role for education to play in the creation of "human capital"' (2.1). Fortunately, though, there have been some 'recent advances in growth theory'. These new theories have (italics added) *proposed ... mechanisms whereby education affects productivity levels*' but they

> typically incorporate ... *crucial assumptions [the] empirical basis [of which] is essentially unknown* ... Firms are *assumed* not to be able fully to appropriate the gains from the production of knowledge so that spillovers occur. ('Growth Theory')

There are three types of new theory: '"sources of growth" equation models', an 'augmented "Solow" or neo-classical model' and 'endogenous growth models'. Unfortunately, only the third allows for crumbs (2.7, 2.13–14). Moreover, although it does make an 'assumption' that would 'allow' them to be 'inferred' (2.14),

> identifying the existence and extent of education
> externalities ... is ... fraught with difficulties ... and, until
> the methodologies and data used in empirical studies are
> developed further, all results should be treated with caution.
> (3.3)

And that's the sum total of the theoretical justification for the £6 billion a year of taxes that goes on the universities.

B. The evidence

DIRECT OR EXPERIMENTAL

There is none.

> To identify HE externalities we ... need to observe the
> productivity of 'uneducated' workers with and without the
> presence of their HE-educated colleagues. Unfortunately
> such controlled experiments are almost never possible. (1.7)

INDIRECT

In the absence of direct experimental evidence, we have to rely on inferences made from large-scale statistical comparisons between economies with more and less developed higher education systems. These might be comparisons between the economies of different countries ('cross-country') or between earlier and later stages in the development of the economy of a single country ('time-series').

(A) FINDINGS

There is some tentative evidence that [there] may [be] indicati[ons of] possible externalities.

OECD countries which expanded their higher education more rapidly ... experienced faster growth. The direction of causation however is unclear.

The only specific group of graduates which have been examined for productivity growth effects are 'scientists and engineers'.

There is some evidence that education affects physical capital investment ... which ... raises income growth rates, though the specific role of higher education is less clear.

There is increasing evidence that research and development activities may be important for productivity growth and ... spillover ... The additional link from higher education to research and development (R&D) is yet to be confirmed but some evidence is beginning to suggest that HE may be important.

The most direct evidence on HE externalities comes from comparisons of macro and micro rate of return estimates. There are currently very few of the former, but present evidence suggests, at most, very modest upward revision of standard social rates of return to account for externalities. ('Empirical Evidence')

(B) WARNINGS

(I) GENERAL WARNINGS (italics original)

data *quality* that is very different ... and ... proxy variables (of varying degrees of accuracy) [are used] because conceptually more appropriate variables are not available. (3.6)

A particular problem concerns human capital measurement. To capture the production externalities of higher education it is clearly necessary to have an accurate measure of the extent to which HE augments the quality of labour input. However, measuring the output of education in general, and HE in particular, is notoriously difficult. As a result input measures tend to be used ... It is very difficult to know how close these proxies are to their conceptual equivalents. (3.7)

The cross-section regression methodology is a useful means of identifying *correlations* between variables of interest (e.g. HE and income growth) ... It is less good at identifying *causation* from one variable to another, and most regression studies make prior assumptions regarding causality with, at best, limited testing of these assumptions. (3.8)

(II) WARNINGS ABOUT CROSS-COUNTRY COMPARISONS

One 'strange' finding of 'the most comprehensive evidence from cross-section regressions' is that 'female education (both secondary and tertiary) appears to be inversely related to growth' (3.11): another study throws up the 'puzzle' that although 'the number of scientists and engineers per capita is found to be significant ... similarly strong effects for years of university educational attainment' are not (3.12); and then another couple of studies 're-port cross-section regression results in which educational attainment variables appear to be negatively related to growth' (3.15). Professor Gemmell sums up this section:

> Cross-section regression studies of growth have numerous
> methodological drawbacks and much more testing on better
> quality educational data, particularly for higher education,
> is required before firm conclusions can be drawn on the
> direct effect of education on economic growth. (3.19)

He does immediately go on to say, 'In my view, the weight of evidence is increasingly that education is positively associated with income growth, and higher education seems to to be the most important variable' (3.19). But, as he has already himself pointed out, this does nothing to explain income growth; there is no claim to have established a 'direction of causality'. All it tells us is that when people have a lot of money they often have a lot of education (the same goes for wine).

(III) WARNINGS ABOUT 'TIME-SERIES' COMPARISONS

This kind of study is 'potentially more reliable ... not least because it avoids the questionable assumptions implicit in much cross-country work'. Unfortunately, 'in practice, limited numbers of observations often restricts [sic] the use of time-series methods (or their sophistication) and to date there are few studies of this sort' (3.20).

C. Conclusion

> The evidence ... for educational externalities (and
> especially for those associated with higher education) is still
> very limited in scope and extent. Any conclusions ... must be
> regarded as tentative, not least because the quality of both
> the available data and testing methodologies are [sic] ...
> flawed. (4.4)

So there you are. Everything is tentative and uncertain – theory, data, methods, conclusions. It's all guesswork. And what do you call an investment based on guesswork? A gamble? Well, you might, except that in this case the government goes on betting, year after year, with our money, without having any idea whether we're winning or losing. What independent financial advisor would recommend that the Chancellor put his own money where he puts our taxes? And if one did, what prudent Chancellor would take his advice?

If no 'externalities' can be reliably identified, then, in Professor Gemmell's words, 'there is no immediate economic case for subsidising the HE system. State-funded education [is] merely taxing some individuals (with resulting efficiency losses) in order to enhance the private gains to others ... a socially wasteful investment' – that is, no investment at all. The entire state-subsidised expansion of higher education, maintained by so many governments over so many years, with no semblance of justification offered for it that isn't economic, has been, it seems, a tremendous error, economically. And if the subsidies were withdrawn, the grotesquely bloated system they have created would shrink back to something that made economic (and educational) sense. The so-called customers would be found simply not to exist and the so-called need for this so-called education would vanish with them. In its present shape and size the whole thing is simply a creation of wastefulness. And that's according to what is in effect the government's own economic adviser, advising a government which, like all its recent predecessors, can't imagine any case for higher education that isn't economic. An investment? It's not even a bet. It's like throwing money over your shoulder and wishing.

It isn't just the fact that it has been subsidised through the taxes that makes the fifteen-or-more-fold expansion of the higher education system an error. It would still be an economic error, however it were funded. The case for it depends on two assumptions (made as a matter of routine by Sausman and Steel but questioned by Gemmell), which any ordinarily prudent investor would want to query: that people with degrees are more productive than those without and that it is their education which makes them so. Research is supposed to be one of the things that make universities an investment. How much research into the productivity conferred by the degrees they award have they ever undertaken?

How would you measure how much more productive a graduate was than a non-graduate? As Professor Gemmell says, you'd have to observe the two performing similar tasks and see whether the graduates were more efficient. But, as he also says, 'Measuring the output of education in general, and HE in particular, is notoriously difficult' (3.7) and 'controlled experiments are almost never possible' (1.7). So the way economists do it is simply by taking the greater income of graduates as a measure of greater productivity: they measure, that is, how much more someone contributes to the economy by measuring how much more he takes from it (his net wages plus whatever else he costs his employer – taxes and national insurance and pension contributions) and treat the one as a proxy for the other. Now this, however scientific a practice, does produce in Report 7 some odd effects of language:

> the economic benefits from graduates ... their higher earnings (1)
>> the contribution graduates make to the economy ... the high salaries ... they receive (1.1)

These are the wonderland phrases Dearing is echoing when he says, 'Society benefits from higher education to the extent that a graduate [earns] a greater amount post-tax'. If this is how graduates benefit society, it must be more blessed to give than to receive in ways Jesus never dreamt of. Who in his right mind would agree to subsidise someone else's education for the somebody else to get more pay than himself? What ordinary employer thinks a wage increase in itself evidence of an increase in productivity? How many shareholders think the mere fact that their directors award one another big bonuses proves that those big bonuses have been earned? (*Not*, apparently, the big investment houses, which have become very annoyed about it.) It's logic through the looking-glass.

Pay may make, as Sausman and Steel call it, 'a straightforward measure' of productivity, but only in the sense that it is straightforward to make; it's hardly straightforward to think. Do we get what we pay for? Well, perhaps we do, but hardly as surely as we pay for what we get. All an employer can know is whether he is paying the going rate or not; the connection between that rate and the relative productivity of employees of different levels of education is as opaque to him as to any economist, and for the same reason: the experiments that would make it demonstrable can't be performed. The graduate wants more money for his higher qualification and to make up for his lost earnings; the employer is willing to give it him; and they settle, on average, for a certain sum. And that, in the absence of direct comparative evidence, is all that is known; and to know anything more is made all the harder by the fact that a great many jobs that graduates do are not open to non-graduates, so there is no direct competition. Nobody knows what part mere custom plays in setting such differentials.

But even if graduates could be shown to be more productive, it still wouldn't follow that it was their education that made them so. As Professor Gemmell says,

> There is a very credible economics literature which suggests that education (including higher education) may be no more than a screening device which allows employers to identify the more able potential employees from the rest. Thus graduates' wages are higher because they are inherently more productive, for example because they work harder or have more innate ability, but not because they are better educated. If this is the case then the current system of HE may simply be providing employers with a privately cheap, but socially expensive (i.e. wasteful), screening system. If firms know that the most productive individuals will choose to go to (state-subsidised) university, then they will select graduates in preference to non-graduates even if education has no effect on their productivity. Likewise, 18 year olds go to university to signal to employers that they are productive. There may still be a case for governments subsidising this 'screening system' if alternative screening devices are less efficient and if there are adverse social consequences from the mismatches which might result, such as unemployment or high labour turnover. However it is quite possible, if employers and/or employees had to fully fund a screening system privately, that they would be able to devise something more efficient than the current HE system. (1.2)

Sausman and Steel acknowledge that it may be difficult to be sure how far it is a graduate's education rather than something else about him which makes him more productive (if he is), but they make their uncertainty a pretext for more calculations which any competent auditor would suspect. They rephrase Professor Gemmell's question 'How can we know whether it is education that does the trick or not?' as 'How much of the trick does education do?' or, in their own terms, what is the correct value for the *alpha* factor? (1.8–1.12 and Table 2.1; also Annexe A, 'Measuring the Social Rate of Return', 3, 11 and Tables 1–3).

The alpha *factor?*

Sausman and Steel first of all suppose that the higher productivity of a graduate can be portioned up like the higher wages which are supposed to measure it and each portion attributed to a separate, distinguishable cause: so much to family background, so much to innate ability, so much to education, etc. These causes are named 'factors'; 'research' assigns each a numerical value; and education is singled out from them all to be distinguished as *alpha*. Sausman and Steel then talk about 'the *alpha* factor' in the tones of scientists investigating something as ordinarily and verifiably real as the stone Dr Johnson kicked in attempted refutation of Berkeley: 'Given the empirical uncertainties over the value of *alpha*, we present results for *alpha* values of 0.6 and 0.8', that is, we are going to attribute between 60 per cent and 80 per cent of the higher productivity of graduates, which we have inferred from their higher wages, to their education – renamed 'level of human capital' (Annexe A, 11). But this is just verbal magic, mumbo-jumbo, superstition in a modern form. Why do they make this attribution? Where do they get their 0.6 and 0.8 from? These figures are 'suggested by the available research evidence' – Annexe A, 11. (Oh, that's all right, then.) But wouldn't someone intending to risk his money on a new company with their 60–80 per cent in mind ('We must have graduates because of their much greater productivity') want to know how 'evidence' so scanty and imprecise could support figures so exact, and so large?

Conclusion

So who is right – those who like Sausman and Steel think that the education that graduates receive makes them more productive – 'creates human capital' – or those others who think it is merely a 'screening device'? To give the crucial words of Professor Gemmell a little more fully:

> So, is it possible to discriminate between 'human capital' and 'screening' arguments in any systematic way . . . ? Ideally one would hope to observe workers with different levels of education (but otherwise identical) undertaking similar tasks and see whether the more educated performed these tasks more efficiently . . . Unfortunately such controlled experiments are almost never possible. (1.7)

And that is Professor Gemmell's last word on the subject. How can we know whether education makes people more productive or not? We can't. We just don't know in any way that economists understand knowledge. But we invest billions every year on the assumption that we can and do know, all the same. On that assumption we have already increased the numbers in higher education from 1 in 33 to more than 1 in 3. On that assumption Gordon Brown proposes increasing them to 1 in 2 (*Today* programme, 16 June 2000).

If this is investment, put your money under the mattress.

Except that you can't. For this sure-fire, can't-fail investment scheme is run by the government, and participating in it is compulsory, by law. This is an 'investment' the evasion of which is a crime.

9 DREAMING SPIRES AND SPEEDING MODEMS[1]

Niall Ferguson

Disraeli – who had not himself been to one – once called the university 'a place of light, liberty and learning'. As one contemplates the future of British universities today, there is a temptation to shorten that to just 'a place of light learning'.

It was nearly 40 years ago, in the wake of the Robbins Report on Higher Education, that Kingsley Amis made his gloomy prophecy: 'More means worse.' He little knew how much more and how much worse.

Back then, no more than 5 per cent of school leavers went to university. By 1980 the proportion had trebled. But the real 'Big Bang' has come since the 1992 Further and Higher Education Act, which increased the proportion to 30 per cent within three years. That meant an awful lot more students: from around 300,000 in the early sixties to 1.6 million in the nineties. It also meant a lot more universities: from 31 to 115, an expansion facilitated by the decision simply to 'rebrand' the polytechnics. And this revolution is not over. Present policies – remember 'Education, education, education'? – suggest that within the foreseeable future nearly half of all school leavers will go on to university.

But why exactly has more meant worse? One reason is the obvious proposition that the average student is likely to be less capa-

---

1   An earlier and shorter version of this chapter was first published in the *Financial Times*, 4 November 2000.

ble when half of all school leavers go to a university than when the proportion was 1 in 20, unless one believes that the élitism of the past had nothing whatever to do with intellectual ability. The other better argument is that state funding for higher education has lagged far behind the expansion of university places.

It is often forgotten that government funding for English universities began with the Committee on Grants to University Colleges back in 1889. It had already risen to around 40 per cent of total income as early as 1939. But the 1960s were the high tide, when government funds accounted for some 90 per cent of total higher education spending.

Today, by contrast, the typical university gets only around two-thirds of its income from the state in the form of its recurrent grant, Research Council money and fees. (Oxford and Cambridge are different, partly because of the colleges' ancient endowments, which account for around 15 per cent of Oxford's university and college income, but mainly because they find it easier to attract external research grants, which have increased fivefold in real terms since 1965.)

At the same time as government funding has dwindled, state control has limited the universities' freedom. The fees my university charges average around £6,000 per annum, less than half the amount charged for comparable degree courses by MIT, Yale or Harvard (in the neighbourhood of £14,000). At the same time, nationwide academic pay scales – a real relic of the planned economy – make it impossible for British universities to compete with their American counterparts when it comes to hiring the best staff. Indeed, British academic salaries have lagged so far behind comparable salaries in both the public and private sectors that the universities can no longer hope to retain more than a fraction of their best students. The next generation of British academics will have one thing in common, it seems: economic irrationality.

The implications are not difficult to discern. In a recent edition of Oxford University's in-house magazine, Bruce Charlton, a lecturer in psychology at Newcastle, painted a depressing picture of the near future in most British universities. The implicit policy, Charlton argued, is to make universities mass-produce middle managers just as grammar schools used to mass-produce clerks: 'the job', as he put it, 'is to train half the work-force to a not particularly high level'. So in the future, there will be no need for lecturers to pursue independent research: they will simply be glorified schoolteachers. Exams will give way to continuous assessment. Students will no longer fail; they will simply plod on until they have accumulated the requisite number of credits.

'State-funded universities will be characterised by chronic under-funding,' Charlton concluded grimly, 'with disaffected staff, large classes, no individual attention, crowded and run-down facilities. ... It will take until age twenty-one to reach an intellectual level that many pupils used to achieve at sixteen ... The majority of university academics will become school teachers for grown-ups.'

To my mind, the only odd thing about this analysis is that it is couched in the future rather than the present tense.

In the face of Amis's Law, it is of course tempting to retreat into a gloomy nostalgia for the good old days. Many academics do this. Indeed, there are times when I think the ancient graces of the Oxford and Cambridge colleges might as well be replaced by a weary incantation of '*O tempora, O mores.*'

This temptation to mourn the vanished golden age should be resisted, however. Apart from anything else, the past of the English universities was not all golden. Their undoubted achievements in the late nineteenth and twentieth centuries should be contrasted with their parlous condition in the eighteenth, when (unlike in Scotland) the best scholarship was to be found far from the universities. Gibbon famously dismissed his time at Oxford as 'the most idle and unprofitable of my whole life', and the suspicion that the place was little more than a cross between an Anglican seminary and a wine cellar persisted well into the Victorian era. Thomas Carlyle was right when he declared: 'The true University of these days is a collection of books.' Karl Marx did not need a professorial chair to write *Capital* (though perhaps giving him one might have improved it, or at least made it shorter); just a seat in the British Library.

The moral of the story, however, is not that the universities will eventually recover from their recent malaise. They cannot all hope to do so. Even the remedy of privatisation favoured by James Tooley would surely kill almost as many universities as it would cure. While it is clear that Oxford and Cambridge would benefit from weaning themselves off state funding and could expect gradually to build up an Ivy League-style culture of fund-raising and alumni benefactions, this is hardly an option for (to take one example) cash-strapped Edinburgh.

And even Oxford may find it hard. The combined college endowments are dwarfed by Harvard's accumulated capital; and the cost of maintaining Oxford's much older buildings swallows up much of the colleges' income. Nor am I convinced that it will be easy to foster the culture of the alumnus bountiful so crucial to Ivy League finances.

Long years of state funding have blinded even supposedly intelligent Oxford undergraduates to the unsustainability of the old 'free degrees' system. I occasionally point out to my students that they could expect an average annual return (after tax and in real terms) of at least 10 per cent on their university education if they had to pay for it themselves, and that therefore they *should* pay for it themselves. Even if they had to borrow the lot it would still be a good investment. This usually elicits the response that poor sixth-formers would be deterred from going to university by an American-style system of funding. Yet the present system of state funding subsidises not the poor but the rich (state spending per person on higher education is five times higher for people in the top fifth of income than for those in the bottom fifth). And it is far from clear that a transparent system of fees accompanied by a serious system of scholarships would deliver a less equal outcome than the current British system, which is in fiscal terms regressive.

But these arguments are hard to sell. When they are at university, my students feel themselves to be poor and regard debts of £10,000 as oppressive. When they leave and begin earning salaries that dwarf their student debts, they feel no sense of obligation to their alma mater. And why should they? Graduates whose degrees have been paid for by the state are primarily indebted to the state, and regard a 40 per cent higher income tax rate as repayment enough.

Yet the future of the universities is not all decline and fall. While the established universities – and especially the redbricks – lumber on like the starving giant herbivores in the last episode of the television series *Walking with Dinosaurs*, new and more sprightly institutions are evolving that portend an altogether rosier future for higher education.

The Internet was, of course, originally intended as a means to facilitate academic communication. Since its inception it has experienced a gold-rush style invasion by 'e-tailers' and others. But as the e-commerce bubble deflates, the World Wide Web shows signs of rediscovering its academic roots.

As a way of simply communicating ideas, the Internet is as revolutionary as the printing press. For example, it can take between three months and a year for an article to pass from submission to publication in a printed scholarly journal. But the Internet allows researchers to get papers into the public domain instantly, even while the journal referees are dithering with their reports. It has also made the task of collaboration between scholars in different institutions far easier than in the past. Now drafts of joint papers or even whole books can be batted back and forth across the Atlantic in a matter of seconds. Above all, the Web makes an ever-growing quantity of electronic resources – ranging from immense databases of economic statistics to libraries of medieval iconography – accessible to anyone with a computer, a modem and a phone socket.

Of course, Amis's Law holds good here too. In the on-line world as on earth itself, more has meant worse. Because there are next to no entry barriers, any madman can establish a website on any subject, and if he calls its 'World_war_two.com' then the chances are that your search for material on 'World War Two' will turn up his site – along with between two hundred thousand and a million other websites, depending on which search engine you use. But it is possible to sift the wheat from the vast quantities of chaff. Last year I helped launch Boxmind, an on-line company designed to sort and rate academic resources on the Internet so that students and lecturers can easily find the tens of thousands of valuable resources that are 'out there', but buried.

The question I have been asking myself for several years remains: could initiatives like Boxmind lead eventually to the creation of a virtual university or e-versity?

Of course, 'distance learning' is already thriving in many parts of the world. There are, according to one estimate, around eleven 'mega-universities' with more than 100,000 enrolled students apiece, the biggest of which is DIANDA, the China Television University, which has a total enrolment of around 850,000 (compare that with Oxford's 15,000).

But these are really television universities like our own Open University, supported by traditional correspondence courses. The e-university is a different proposition, using the Internet to allow more immediate interaction between teacher and student. Now that broadband technology is becoming more and more widely available – especially in terrestrial universities – it is possible to imagine complete courses in many subjects being delivered in the form of on-line lectures and tutorials. Indeed, such courses already exist in the US. And from September British universities will be able to subscribe to Boxmind 'e-lectures', which will allow their students to see and hear some of the most eminent academics in the world, including Richard Dawkins, Ronald Dworkin, Steven Pinker, Martin Rees, Ian Stewart and Bernard Williams.

This is the future, and I am certain it works, not least because it allows the lecturer to import many of the best techniques of documentary television, without having to dumb down the content for a mass TV audience. Yet the audience for top-quality e-lectures is potentially huge precisely because the Internet is international. Add together all the people around the world working towards university level qualifications and you have a potentially enormous – dare I say it? – market.

Do developments like this portend extinction for the terrestrial universities? It is perhaps tempting to picture the redbricks finally keeling over like famished brontosaurs, while a new breed of private e-versities inherits the earth like the first mammals.

Nevertheless, it seems to me that the old and the new in this case may turn out to be complementary rather than competitors. That is certainly the Oxford view. Plans are now afoot to pool resources with Princeton, Stanford and Yale with a view to providing virtual lectures and other on-line resources to alumni – all part of the new post-graduation service.

The combination is an unlikely one: dreaming spires and speeding modems. Yet if the alternative is the dystopia predicted by Kingsley Amis – of mass-produced mediocrity in the name of 'anti-élitism' – then the best hope of preserving academic excellence may well lie in just such a marriage of ancient and modern.

Who knows? This time the dinosaurs and mammals might just be able to coexist.

10 THE UNIVERSITY OF BUCKINGHAM: AN HISTORICAL PERSPECTIVE
John Clarke

Compared to many other occupations, the academic life may seem a solitary one, but, in some respects, academics are social animals. They draw together for mutual protection, forming academic guilds as defensive bulwarks against an outside world that is at best suspicious and at worst downright hostile. The 'Town', that is the non-academic world, is never to be trusted; pity the poor Gowns-man in medieval Oxford without a university to protect him. The essential thing about guilds, especially academic guilds – otherwise known as universities – is that they are self-governing. They are given the privilege of running their own affairs by some outside and ultimately superior body. In earlier times, that outside body was a municipality or the Church; latterly it has been the state. The privileges of a university are enshrined in a legal document, a Charter, that defines the nature of its independence and sets up the institutional arrangements through which it is to operate.

There is a potential for conflict between privileged guild and outside authority. If a university effectively repudiates the authority of the grantor of its Charter, it becomes answerable only to itself. Hence, it acquires the essential attribute of sovereignty; it becomes an academic city-state. It develops institutions similar to those of other states – its own legal system, police force and frontiers. Of course, not all those who live or work within its territory will be academics; even an academic city-state needs the services of the Town. But the Gowns-men rule and the Towns-men are their subjects. Any suggestion that Town knows better than Gown – and can thus tell it how to run its affairs – appears ridiculous and against nature.

In moments of solitary reflection, even today's academics may find the idea of an academic city-state appealing. Yet few have enough self-confidence to believe that they should be truly self-governing. The Town is only too ready to agree. What are the sources of this self-doubt? Edward Gibbon's *Autobiography* is a likely culprit. Readers will know that an academic city-state is not a complete fantasy; rather it is based upon the supposed reality of eighteenth-century Oxford. Quite literally, it is a sobering thought. Were not Gibbon's 'Monks of Magdalen' steeped in 'port and prejudice'? More than anyone else, Gibbon is responsible for an enduring stereotype – the lazy, self-indulgent don, the sort who 'well remembered that he had a salary to receive, but only forgot he had a duty to perform'.[1] If that was the way academics were when left to their own devices, then they needed to be controlled. Gibbon's case against the academic city-state is couched in the language of the free market:

> The legal incorporation of these societies by the charters of
> popes and kings had given them a monopoly of the public
> instruction; and the spirit of monopolists is narrow, lazy
> and oppressive: their work is more costly than that of
> independent artists; and new improvements so eagerly
> grasped by the competition of freedom, are admitted with

---

1   Bury, J. B. (ed.), *Autobiography of Edward Gibbon, as originally edited by Lord Sheffield,* Oxford University Press, London, 1962, p. 44.

> slow and sullen reluctance in those proud corporations,
> above fear of a rival, and below the confession of an error.
> We may scarcely hope that any reformation will be a
> voluntary act; and so deeply are they rooted in law and
> prejudice, that even the omnipotence of Parliament would
> shrink from an inquiry into the state and abuses of the two
> Universities.[2]

In reality, eighteenth-century Oxford was neither as lazy nor as self-indulgent as Gibbon or his near-contemporary – Adam Smith – claimed, but they had a point. Institutions answerable only to themselves are liable to become corrupt. Although Gibbon doubted whether Parliament would summon up enough courage to tackle the problem, he gives a broad hint that this was the only possible solution.

Has the story of the past 150 years fulfilled Gibbon's programme or has it negated it? Nineteenth-century parliaments displayed more courage than Gibbon anticipated. They asserted their ultimate control over the Ancient Universities in the Royal Commissions of the 1850s and broke their monopolies by granting Royal Charters to a number of new universities. But things did not go too far. Universities made few financial demands on the state and funded themselves from a combination of student fees and the income from their endowments. Hence, state intervention and regulation – from an academic perspective, interference – remained modest.

But things were changing. In the course of the 20th century, universities became increasingly dependent upon the financial support of the state. Thus the state acquired the right and perhaps

---

2   Ibid, p. 37.

the duty to make sure that its money was well spent; that was but a short step to stipulating *how* it should be spent. The danger now was the exact opposite to that found in Gibbon's picture of Oxford. The privileges and independence of the academic guild might disappear. A guild without some privileges and independence is not a guild at all. By the standards of the eighteenth century, everything would become topsy-turvy; Town would rule Gown and Gowns-men would be subjected to Towns-men. Perhaps, above all, state control might become so strong that the state would actually run universities. But there is only one state and a state-run university system would be a monopoly, and a nationalised monopoly at that. Such a prospect would not have appealed either to Smith or to Gibbon.

Perhaps the alarm bells should have rung earlier, but they did not. Few in the universities, even those later associated with the independent university project, objected until it was almost too late. Although the trend towards state control, towards *de facto* nationalisation, was strong, it was still gradual and low profile. Governments of all persuasions sought to maintain an illusion of university independence, and most academics were willing to connive at the deception. Unlike in such industries as coal, the railways, gas or electricity, there was never a single piece of legislation that nationalised the universities. Perhaps it would have been better if there had been. That would have concentrated minds. It is striking that most of the industries subjected to formal nationalisation have subsequently been returned to the private sector, whereas those that experienced 'informal nationalisation' have generally remained under public ownership.

From 1919, at least, the expansion of the university sector seemed to be desirable. But where was the money to come from?

Despite the considerable wealth of many Oxford and Cambridge colleges, they did not possess sufficient resources to finance such an undertaking and, in any case, their incomes were often depressed by prolonged periods of agricultural depression. The money would have come from outside the sector. Logically there were three possibilities – increased fees, large benefactions from private individuals or companies, or funding from the state. Higher fees appeared self-defeating, because that would reduce the number of students and thus prevent the desired expansion. They would make universities more rather than less socially exclusive – a subject upon which some academics were beginning to develop tender consciences. Private or company benefactions were a possibility but would they be sufficient? Taxation regimes were becoming increasingly unfavourable to such gifts. That seemed to leave the state.

But even if private or business funding had been available, would academics have wanted it? For most of the 20th century, the culture of universities was profoundly anti-business. Left and right were at one. The left, increasingly sympathetic to socialism and Marxism, regarded capitalism with hatred. The right favoured Tory state paternalism and regarded businessmen with contempt. Both sides read their Coleridge and their Matthew Arnold; they were the cultured 'clerisy' and businessmen mere 'Philistines', uncultured and ultimately not very clever. Few academics encouraged their brighter students to go into business – though an exception was sometimes made in favour of banking. The best they hoped to keep for themselves while they pointed the good 2:1 sorts to the professions – to the law and above all to the Civil Service. Most academics felt easier in the company of bureaucrats than with commercial types of all descriptions. In both World

War I and World War II many academics became civil servants. On the whole, they found the experience congenial. Some even entertained a more grandiose fantasy than that of the academic city-state. They thought that academics disguised as civil servants could take over the national state.

It might have been expected that such views would be confined to benighted historians and classicists; surely the economists would have rejected such nonsense. But they did not; on the contrary, many were ardent advocates of it. Academic economists – not that there were many of them – were most business-friendly in the middle of the nineteenth century, before the expansion of the university sector became a serious issue. It became a serious issue at precisely the time when academic economic thinking was becoming less friendly to business. If academics were not entirely to be trusted to run universities, there was even less reason to trust businessmen to run business. They too must accept state regulation and direction, accept that the state knew their job better than they did. After all, if the state was to be run by dons in disguise, how could mere businessmen hope to rival their god-like intellects? If not exactly Marxist, such a cast of mind was definitely Keynesian. The state was the key to progress in the economic, social and educational spheres.

But by the end of the 1960s, there were finally signs of alarm. More students were being taught, more universities and polytechnics set up, more public money spent, but were things really getting better, were standards higher than in the past or in foreign countries, were taxpayers really getting a good deal, or the students, or the academics themselves? Some who asked these questions were forced to pessimistic conclusions. The answer was obvious – to go back to first principles and to form a new guild of scholars and students subject to far less state control than had become the norm in the university sector. Ultimately it was this response that was to lead to the establishment of the University of Buckingham.

All institutions are coloured by the circumstances of their foundation. Buckingham's critics have sometimes described it as a reactionary institution. It does represent a reaction against what appeared to be the dominant trends of the late 1960s and early 1970s, trends affecting the economy, politics, culture and life in general. But those who support such a reaction will come from a variety of backgrounds. They may be united in disapproving of what is but find it harder to agree on what should be. At the risk of some oversimplification, the project for an independent university was supported by two distinct agendas – the Economic Agenda and the Academic Agenda.

When the word 'independent' is introduced, it is wise to ask 'independent from what?' Supporters of the Economic Agenda would have no hesitation in saying that they meant 'independent from the state'. There can be no doubt of the close links between Buckingham and the revival of free-market economics, applied to virtually all areas of activity. This was exemplified in the involvement of a man like Ralph Harris in both the IEA and the project for an independent university. For economists of this sort, the crucial thing about higher education was that it had become a monopoly, and a nationalised monopoly at that. In higher education, as in other areas, nationalised monopolies have their drawbacks. The essence of a monopoly is that there is no real competition, the essential spur to an improving product. Monopolies are 'producer led'. They offer what they think the customer should want – on a 'take it or leave it' basis. Nationalised monopolies are even worse. There are constant changes of policy, lack of clarity about objectives – especially whether social and political considerations should influence management decisions – and of course growing red tape. Staff become state bureaucrats. Above all, nationalised monopolies are inefficient, offering poor value for money to their ultimate 'shareholders', the taxpayers.

The first economic argument for an independent university is that it will introduce competition into higher education. Secondly, it will reduce bureaucracy and avoid the conflicting priorities inherent in nationalised industries. Thirdly, the pressures of the market would force it to utilise its resources more efficiently than its state-subsidised rivals. Finally, an independent university will derive its income and pay its staff from student fees rather than from state subsidies. It will be a business, or at any rate like a business, because it will depend upon its customers and have to put their needs and preferences first.

It follows from the Economic Agenda that while an independent university will be independent of the state, it will be dependent upon the market. Gibbon may have hinted that the state should exercise more control over Oxford but he was more explicit about the need for control by the market. Appealing to 'the positive and impartial evidence of a master of moral and political wisdom', he asserts:

> Dr Smith assigns as the cause of their indolence, that
> instead of being paid by voluntary contributions, which
> would urge them to increase the number, and to deserve the
> gratitude of their pupils, the Oxford professors are secure in
> the enjoyment of a fixed stipend, without the necessity of
> labour or the apprehension of control.[3]

3   Ibid, p. 38.

The ultimate source of these fixed stipends are endowments, and it follows that in a full-blooded independent but market-dominated university the main, and perhaps the only, source of income will be fees. But there was more to it than that. The market requires efficiency; sellers want to maximise revenue in relation to costs and buyers want to keep prices down. Both point to the desirability of new methods of teaching:

> It has been observed, nor is the observation absurd, that excepting in experimental sciences, which demand a costly apparatus and a dextrous hand, the many valuable treatises that have been published on every subject of learning may now supersede the ancient mode of oral instruction.[4]

In other words, new technology – in this case books but by implication further advances as well – might render traditional face-to-face teaching redundant. Yet Gibbon hesitates about this conclusion. Lectures are still needed, if only because, without them, idle students may learn nothing at all:

> But there still remains a material difference between a book and a professor; the hour of the lecture enforces attendance; attention is fixed by the presence, the voice, and the occasional questions of the teacher; the most idle will carry something away; and the more diligent will compare the instructions which they have heard in the school, with the volumes which they peruse in their chamber.[5]

Yet the importance of fees and of teaching raises the difficult question of where research and publications come in. Gibbon

---

4   Ibid.
5   Ibid, p. 39.

sidesteps this, but he implies that publications are to be regarded as by-products of teaching and hence secondary to it:

> Whatever science he professes he may illustrate in a series of discourses, composed in the leisure of his closet,
> pronounced on public occasions, and finally delivered to the press.[6]

The points made by Gibbon are of direct relevance to the Economic Agenda for an independent university. Ideally, if the university is to derive its income from fees and not rely on endowments, the fees it charges must be lower than those prevailing in other institutions and/or the quality of its teaching product must be markedly superior. The problem will be especially acute if the fees at rival institutions are subsidised by the state. Then there must be truly heroic efforts made to achieve overall competitiveness. The ideal arrangement is to establish a university in the centre of a large city – probably London – to maximise the numbers of students who could save on living costs by remaining at home. Plant will have to be worked intensively – certainly throughout the year, and perhaps on a shift basis with lectures and tutorials scheduled through the night. Every advantage of modern technology must be taken to allow a less generous staff-student ratio without any loss of overall quality. But even then the academic staff may have to accept a heavier burden of teaching – involving unsocial hours and perhaps unsocial times of the year – than their colleagues in the state sector. The time available for research is likely to be 'squeezed'. It must be stressed that, individually, few if any of those who subscribed to the Economic Agenda advocated all these

---

6   Ibid.

features. But they do represent the sum total of the analysis. Couched in such stark terms there seems little about this agenda to attract anyone actually contemplating seeking employment at the proposed independent university. Although the state system's most distinctive feature is that it subsidises students, in reality it also protects academics from market forces. Those who are the beneficiaries of such protection rarely wish to forgo it.

But that does not mean that the idea had no appeal at all. Many academics resented the prospect of becoming bureaucrats, trying – probably in vain – to keep up with the vagaries of state policy. That was not the way they had planned to spend their lives. Some feared that political considerations would soon influence selection policy, even what was taught and how it was interpreted. Academic freedom was at stake. Academics must have the freedom to explore and express unconventional views – strange to some and perhaps even repugnant to much of the rest of society. There was a danger too that courses were becoming too similar in state universities. Some, especially people like Max Beloff, thought that courses were becoming too specialised and narrow. A broader education, including some study of a foreign language and a science, was essential. There were fears that the desire to maximise student numbers was having an adverse effect on staff–student ratios; the individual attention inherent in the traditional system of tutorials was being stretched to breaking point. Academics were conscious of the fact that many of the new universities and polytechnics erected in the 1960s had been hastily and shoddily built – they frequently resembled the tower blocks of municipal housing which was already causing or exhibiting serious social problems. It was hard to imagine that such squalid environments would encourage higher thoughts.

But it was not just the state and its policies which worried many academics. At least the state could be regarded as an 'external'. The other danger was an internal one. It came from within the guild, from within the curtilage. It took the form of a threat from the academics' own students, even from their own colleagues. Academics know that, while students often claim to be highly individualistic, in reality few groups are more the slaves of fashion – and fashion is essentially anti-individualistic and conformist in the broader sense of the word. In the late 1960s and early 1970s, the fashion was for demonstrations, occupations, even for 'revolution'. Allegedly 'right-wing' or 'fascist' lecturers found themselves subjected to abuse and intimidation. The 'Oxford Revolutionary Socialist Students' were extremely rude about Max Beloff, then Gladstone Professor of Government. There seemed a real danger that student radicals would effectively silence those lecturers whose views they did not share, and even go so far as to dictate course content and interpretation. At the very least they made the normal round of lectures difficult and sometimes impossible.

Some attributed the behaviour of 'revolting students' to a sense of alienation produced by squalid surroundings and a lack of personal contact and proper pastoral care, which was the inevitable result of deteriorating staff–student ratios. Others blamed the pernicious influence of Marxist colleagues, the effects of 'pop culture' or the general decline in respect for authority. While academics may be pleased when students challenge their views, they have strong feelings about the manner in which the challenges should be made. In the last resort, they expect at least a modicum of respect, even of deference, which they believe their status and learning entitles them to. In other words the Academic Agenda involves putting both the state and the students back in their proper places.

But while it was possible to envisage a university in which the state had little or no role, it was much harder to imagine one without students – unless it was possible to attract vast endowments to allow the academics to concentrate exclusively on their research or indeed to live in idleness. However beguiling, such a prospect seemed highly unlikely. If the state was removed from the equation, an independent university – deriving most of its income from fees rather than from state grants – would surely be even more at the mercy of the students than was the case in the state sector. There were perhaps a few who thought, though they did not say so, that the great merit of high fees would be that they would exclude the riff-raff; an independent university would be a university for gentlefolk.

Yet such thoughts, even if they occurred at all, were quite alien to the outlook of most of the academic supporters of the independent university project. Few could be regarded as genuine members of an exclusive social establishment. Many came from quite humble backgrounds and several were Jewish. At least for a while, both Beloff and Harry Ferns had been members of the Communist Party. If no longer the egalitarians they had once been, they were deeply committed to meritocracy and the work ethic. Although often critical of the genuine social exclusivism they had encountered in the 1930s, they were deeply grateful for the opportunities that a university education had afforded them. They valued it all the more because they knew that in terms of their own class they had been a highly privileged minority. What saddened them was that, now that a university education was becoming available to far more people, so many seemed to regard it with contempt. What they really wanted was to create an environment in which students, many from humble backgrounds, would work as they had done in the 1930s. Of course, services that are free or virtually free tend to be despised. If students or their parents had to pay something approaching the economic fees for their courses, they would learn to value them more. Fees would effect the necessary 'reformation of manners' and in some senses 'put the students back in their place'.

Last but not least, many of the academics and other supporters of the project had links with the United States of America. It is striking that the first hint of the idea of an independent university appeared in a letter published in *The Times* in 1968. The author, Dr Paulley, had already become alarmed about medical training in this country. He had just returned from America and experienced private medical schools there. Others who also knew the United States appreciated that, on the other side of the Atlantic, many private colleges and universities were held in high regard, but were not seen as in any way socially divisive or controversial. At least to date, the University of Buckingham has not established a medical school, but Dr Paulley's initiative did point to a significant element in the University's future – the role of the professions.

Depending on one's point of view, the Academic Agenda was either more or less radical than the Economic Agenda. Although it accepted that market forces would be more powerful than in the state sector and produce some beneficial consequences, it did not want to change state control to total control by the market. It was quite prepared to solicit endowments and it valued research. In some cases – certainly in that of Charles Vereker, and perhaps in some facets of Max Beloff's complex personality – there was a streak of nostalgia and of traditionalism, whose inspiration came, if not from the Oxford of the eighteenth century, at least from the Oxford of the 1930s. Their ideal was a learned society in which students, if a little boisterous and enjoying a busy social life – only possible in a residential university – ultimately knew their place. They wanted to keep fees down, but not at the cost of the destruction of traditional tutorial teaching or a depressing physical environment. They thought that an independent university would attract many of its students from famous public schools. They said they regretted this, but perhaps they did not mind too much. They talked of scholarships to attract the less advantaged – something which some 'hardline' Economic Agenda supporters regarded with suspicion. While they wanted independence, they argued that some links with the state sector should be retained – essential for the recognition of qualifications and perhaps for the type of grants that did not have too many strings attached.

When looking at the men and women who turned the project for an independent university into the reality of the University of Buckingham, and then developed it over the past 25 years, these 'agendas' may seem too extreme. There were many, not least the successive Principals and Vice-Chancellors, who tried to keep a foot in both camps. But, underneath it all, the intellectual division was always there and remains to this day. This is not necessarily a criticism – in some ways the tension was fruitful – but it is instructive to consider the story of Buckingham in the light of what each agenda has achieved or failed to achieve, and for what reasons. Here it may be observed that the driving force has been essentially pragmatic – opportunities and adversities – but sometimes this has favoured one tradition and sometimes the other.

In the early days, the Academic Agenda appeared to be in the ascendant. After a false start, Max Beloff was appointed as Principal designate, and Max was essentially an Academic Agenda man. He chose as his deputies Charles Vereker and Caryl Ramsden, and appointed the present author as Dean of Admissions. In retrospect it is clear that we all came into the same camp. But it was not really a matter of personal preference; in the last resort, the Academic Agenda prevailed because it was cheaper and more practical, because, in the circumstances of the 1970s, it was the only way to turn the dream of an independent university into reality. The problem with any institution that intends to rely on fees is that it cannot charge any until it has opened for business. In other words it has to incur start-up costs. Other things being equal, the larger the proposed institution, the longer the period before opening and the greater the start-up costs. Time was passing, and some doubted that the project would ever come to fruition. The Economic Agenda, with its assumption of a city-centre site and thousands of students, implied heavy start-up costs. In the adverse economic circumstances of the early 1970s there was never really any chance that such sums would be available – either as benefactions or as loans. Some money was subscribed but only enough to contemplate beginning on a modest scale. Rural property was cheaper than urban property, and it was probably less expensive to convert existing buildings than to construct new ones. This was the ultimate logic behind the choice of Buckingham as the location for the project – but that meant a residential university with associated expenses. As the conversion work proceeded, the traditional implications became obvious. The old buildings, the river and the ancient town created an overall ambience far more reminiscent of an Oxford college than of a city-centre university. Numbers too were modest – only 46 when the first students arrived in 1976. The traditional or Academic Agenda was reinforced by Beloff's insistence on a broad syllabus with compulsory languages and science for all students. If numbers were modest and benefactions limited there could be no chance that Buckingham could compete with the subsidised state sector. It was pointless to try. The only possible course was to justify high fees by stressing factors like more personal attention, more generous staff–student ratios and more agreeable environment than anything available in the new 'tower block' universities. In other words marketing would have to emphasise the traditional.

But the Economic Agenda had a significant success. It was still necessary to do something to keep student costs down. Students paying high fees were scarcely likely to relish a shift system with midnight tutorials – any more than semi-retired consultant professors with houses in North Oxford would want to give them. But students might be glad of the savings in living costs resulting from a longer academic year, thus enabling them to graduate after two rather than the conventional three years. The two-year degree is probably Buckingham's best-known innovation, but it was 'invented' for this essentially practical reason. Many of the benefits of the system – its appeal to mature students, for example – were appreciated only after it was introduced. A good deal of the 'Buckingham message' was made up as time went on. It was probably none the worse for that, but there was less of a detailed blueprint than some supposed.

Supporters of the Academic Agenda always wanted to retain some links with the state sector. They believed that the best way to gain recognition for the qualifications – obviously essential for the recruitment of students – was through validation from some external academic body. Approaches were made to the Council for National Academic Awards (CNNA), but discussions were broken off when it became clear that validation would not be forthcoming. It was necessary to award 'Licences' to Buckingham's first graduates

– qualifications that appeared to be of rather uncertain status. Of course, from the perspective of the Economic Agenda, market forces would mean that these qualifications would be acceptable if the students who possessed them proved to be good employees. But with the prospect of very small cohorts of graduates, how could the Buckingham Licence become familiar to employers?

In the event a solution was found which in some ways represented a compromise between the philosophies of the Academic and Economic agendas. Perhaps the learned professions represent a halfway house between the world of the market and the world of state regulation. They enjoy substantial independence but in some respects they are monopolies. It is possible that Buckingham came to aspire to be their academic equivalent. The fact that the Law Society and the Bar Council agreed to give the same professional exemptions to holders of Buckingham Licences in law as those accorded to holders of law degrees from other universities probably did more than anything else to enable Buckingham to acquire a reasonable viability. Of course, when the University received its Royal Charter in 1983, the problem was removed – although this could be regarded as a further step in the traditionalist direction.

For most of the University's existence, law students have formed the largest group. Although total numbers have remained modest, never exceeding one thousand, the Law School has reached a sufficient size to have a substantial presence in the academic discipline and in the profession. Although some students were recruited in other areas, the heavy dependence upon law, especially in the early days, had important implications. The two-year degree was particularly attractive to those facing a further period of study and examinations before they could practise. That suggested that further 'professional' courses, such as Accounting, might provide the right way forward. It appeared that many students were willing to pay Buckingham's high fees if they could gain the professional qualifications required for supposedly lucrative careers. They were less willing to pay similar fees for non-vocational courses of a more traditional academic nature. They were also less than enthusiastic about the language and science 'Supporting Courses' favoured by Max Beloff. Although some remain, there has been some erosion in this area.

But there were broader considerations. Buckingham faced a difficult competitive situation. Other universities offered fees that were heavily subsidised and the obvious question was 'why come to Buckingham'? There was the two-year degree argument, the pleasant environment, the personal attention and the high quality of the teaching. But was that likely to be enough? Buckingham had to pay attention to the ratio between applications and places in the university sector as a whole. It was likely to do best in those disciplines – like law – where there was a substantial excess demand. But if it based its academic structure on this calculation alone, it might end up with a very strange mix of courses. In particular it might have to close degree programmes in areas where there was ample provision elsewhere and hence a low demand for places at Buckingham. Over the years, this has led to some painful choices. Some degree programmes – such as Life Sciences – have been terminated, even though they were regarded as central to the academic philosophy of the university. In general the professional and larger degree courses have 'subsidised' the smaller 'non-vocational' ones. Once more this reflects a compromise between the two major agendas.

But there was one feature of Buckingham, already visible in the early days but increasingly significant thereafter, that surprised everyone. This was the composition of the student body. It had been anticipated that the two-year degree would result in a rather larger proportion of mature students than was normal at other universities. That expectation was fulfilled. What was unexpected was the high proportion of non-British nationals. It seems that there had been virtual unanimity in expecting a largely British student body, and courses were designed accordingly. Although British students have usually made up the largest single national group, they have rarely accounted for much over 40 per cent of the total – and in many years less. In retrospect, the reason is obvious. In the state sector, non-British – and later non-EU – students were charged something like an economic fee. It followed that it was in the 'overseas' market that Buckingham was most competitive.

In the early days the bulk of the non-British students tended to come from Commonwealth countries, such as Nigeria, Malaysia or Singapore, and usually possessed a reasonable command of English as at least a second language. More recently there has been an increase in students from non-Commonwealth countries, such as Japan, Taiwan, China and the former communist countries of eastern Europe. Perhaps more surprisingly, there has been significant recruitment, especially in the Business area, from EU countries, notably from Germany. Many of these students have good English, but it has been necessary to provide English-language and foundation courses on a scale not envisaged at the beginning. In short, essentially market considerations have fostered the emergence of Buckingham as an 'international university' – now an important part of its overall image.

From its modest beginning in 1976, Buckingham expanded slowly but steadily until 1994. At that time a student body of 1,500 or even 2,000 by the end of the century seemed realistic. Plans were laid and some financial and staffing commitments made to cater for the expected expansion. But instead of growth there followed two years when numbers stagnated. Then there was a fall, amounting to some 30 per cent, between 1996 and 2000. It appeared that Buckingham had successfully overcome the problems of the 1970s only to encounter a bigger crisis at the start of its second decade. The decline in numbers could be attributed both to expansion in the state sector – especially the grant of university status to former polytechnics – and to the decline in the value of many foreign currencies, especially in the crucial market of the Far East.

Some parts of the University were more adversely affected than others. Numbers in the Business School held up reasonably well. Staff costs were reduced, mostly by natural wastage. New graduate programmes were launched and marketing improved. The University spent heavily on information technology and can claim to have a higher investment per student in this area than any other British university. As a result – aided perhaps by a recognition that standards in the state sector are not what they might be – the situation has improved somewhat in 2001, and numbers are rising once more. At the moment the prevailing mood is one of cautious optimism. Despite the end of Life Science undergraduate teaching, the Diabetes Research Unit is flourishing. While Buckingham academics have quite heavy teaching loads and teach for more weeks of the year than their colleagues elsewhere, many manage to publish extensively and are widely regarded as major figures in their fields.

But has Buckingham succeeded? It can be asserted with some confidence that it has managed to chart a *via media* between the excesses of the independent academic state on the one hand and those of state monopoly on the other. Buckingham is not answerable only to itself. Its Council, which has many distinguished 'outsiders', is the ultimate governing body, and academic standards are monitored, not only by the relevant professions, but also by an active Academic Advisory Council. Many of its students go on to take higher degrees at other universities, and its graduates seem to find employment with relatively little difficulty. Above all, most students are adamant that they find the 'Buckingham Experience' well worth while. In more abstract terms it has achieved a working compromise between the potentially conflicting pressures of the market and of academic integrity and values.

But the fact remains that the Buckingham experiment has had no imitators to date. It remains a small minnow in the large pond of higher education in Britain and the even larger global one that is beginning to emerge. Arguably its main problem is that, throughout, it has been undercapitalised. Although it has done much for itself it remains subject to external forces – especially the huge subsidies given to its competitors – over which it has no control. Some of the early supporters of the independent university project expected that it would totally transform the university sector in the space of a few years. They may have expected too much; Buckingham has achieved much simply by being there for 25 years. The next phase – the phase of expanding the independent sector of higher education and transforming attitudes to it – represents the challenge of the future.

11 PRIVATISING UNIVERSITY EDUCATION
Norman Barry

Despite globalisation and the spread of the market allocation of resources, large swathes of public services in the United Kingdom remain organised under principles more redolent of Stalinist central planning than of a modern free economy. Health and education are the major services subject to the attention of modern political leaders, but all of them seem addicted to the idea that improvements can only come from throwing more public money at them. None sees the solution to consumer dissatisfaction, and falling morale among the practitioners of the services, as likely to come from a radical reorganisation of the way they are delivered.

Privatisation is the only solution, so that a market determines supply, indicates the value of labour employed and maximises individual choice in their delivery.

What is distressing is that antediluvian and atavistic ways of thinking about education should persist at a time when, throughout the rest of the world, especially in undeveloped areas, rapid progress is being made in its provision by private agencies.

What is equally disturbing is the fact that Britain, with its rich historical tradition of private university education, has shown little interest in expanding the private sector here. The University of Buckingham was established in 1976, but there have been no imitators. While it is true that there are other institutions at this level they are mainly of the vocational type. Although it is the case that few these days question the legitimacy and efficiency of private choice in school education up to university entrance (and in private health), not many are prepared to extend the same principle to the tertiary level. People seem willing to accept the state's offering, and increasing class sizes, lack of contact between staff and students and the perceived fact that there is no longer a coincidence between the interests of the professoriate and those of the students have not prompted a desire to promote non-state university education. There is nothing comparable to the range of private tertiary (non-profit) education in the United States, and no attempt to emulate the large range of for-profit institutions that are burgeoning in other parts of the world.

One reason might be consumer ignorance: the degree is nationally accepted as being of a uniform standard wherever it is taken, and in whatever subject it is. Employers regard it as a useful screening device, a convenient indicator of a future employee's potential rather than a mark of intellectual distinction. Yet one feels that this will not last much longer. Despite the system of external examining, people will soon realise that a degree, of any class, is worth more from the established universities than from the former polytechnics now called universities. The laborious nature of external examining, and its low pay rewards, are sufficient deterrents to the rigorous maintenance of a similar standard across all universities. Indeed, in their own screening processes employers are already ranking subjects according to their difficulty: they are more likely to be impressed by a third in nuclear physics than a first in one of the myriad of dubious subjects with 'studies' after their name that have appeared in the last 20 years.

Although they are in the long run decisive, these market-led changes to the structure and performance of universities have had very little effect on the institutions so far. Employer-induced corrections to declining standards in universities will have a commercial significance – tempting them to respond to an extent to the needs of the economic world – but they will do little to change the basic behaviour of the university sector. The quasi-monopoly of the state has produced an insular system of higher education which is immune from the outside world, complacent about its own procedures of self-correction, surviving as the last resort of outdated political ideologies and immune from much of the criticism that less well-protected social institutions regularly have to endure. In many ways the modern university resembles a medieval guild in its internal government and in its capacity to resist radical change. Most obvious is its apparent immunity from the market pressures that now govern the behaviour of other institutions in a modern society.

This privilege seems to be a feature of both the public and private sectors. In America there is a huge voluntary, or non-state, sector in higher education, but its behaviour is little different from that of the public. Indeed, the wealth, in terms of endowments, of the major private universities in America is quite staggering, and no doubt Oxford and Cambridge and the various London institutions would survive unreformed even in a completely privatised world.

But however they are organised, the rationale of universities still perplexes informed observers, and throughout history there had been an endless supply of books and papers, of varying pomposity, with titles like 'The idea of a university' or 'The meaning of higher education'. This debate is not only a result of the occasional questioning of the privileges that universities enjoy, but relates to some fundamental features of a free society: for it is clear that institutions of higher learning are thought to be extremely important in its maintenance. At one level of analysis, an exploration of the role that universities play in the preservation of liberty is irrelevant to their existence. From a purely utilitarian perspective, universities simply exist as necessary institutions in the theory of human capital. People who invest in their own human capital acquire skills and capacities which increase their future market value. All such investment is only made if there is some likelihood of a return, in the form of higher salaries. This has to be sufficient to motivate school leavers to lower their time preferences and resist the allure of immediate employment. In a properly functioning market economy the price system will guarantee the optimal supply of trained personnel for whatever the labour market requires. Any shortfall in labour supply will be followed by higher pay, thus putting out a signal that it is worthwhile for individuals to invest in their human capital. Of course, persons might be deterred by the cost of that investment – fees for courses, and so on – and a society might 'waste' valuable assets if people do not train. But the market would produce an efficient loan system for those who lacked initial resources. Anyway, educational institutions themselves would have every incentive to track down scarce talent and reward it with zero-priced fees and generous cost-of-living allowances.

From a utilitarian perspective, higher education is not an intellectual problem, for the market will always provide an optimal amount of university-trained personnel. Here universities simply respond to supply and demand, and it is not their responsibility to create or to conserve the 'higher' or non-marketable values of education in a free society. This efficiency-based rationale has considerable value, but the debate about higher education concerns more than this. For people value universities for reasons other than their contribution to an efficient labour market. It is for these largely cultural factors that effort is expended in defending the privileges (often protection against competition) of universities in either the public or private sectors. For example, security of tenure is a feature of both public and private sectors in America (it was true of the United Kingdom until quite recently) – a protection for incumbents defended on the ground that it is necessary for academic freedom. Universities are normally relieved of regular tax obligations for the reason that they are not profit-seeking companies but bodies which are providing some kind of public good, from which everybody benefits. For a whole range of reasons universities are thought to be different from other educational institutions. Their rationale is as much cultural as utilitarian.

Universities and a free society

It is because of the importance of liberty as a social value that people argue the case for private universities independent of the state. Most people agree that it would be unwise to depend on the goodwill of state officials for the preservation of freedom of discussion and of research. There has to be some institutional protection for that liberty, some bulwark, importantly in property, which protects individuals from the need to answer to government in whatever they want to do. It is also crucial that such educational bodies should be properly self-governing so that their personnel are not appointed by political authorities, whose agendas are not likely to be dominated by the impartial advancement of knowledge, the preservation of an intellectual tradition or the passing on to future generations of a nation's cultural patrimony.

A private university is today part of what is called *civil society*, that range of autonomous institutions which stand some way between the market and the state. Its component parts are by no means exclusively concerned with economic ends – in fact these days the concept has been seized by those sceptical of the market – but they are characterised by their voluntary nature and genuine self-government. Civil society is well exemplified by churches, but those labour organisations that set up voluntary welfare arrangements in the late nineteenth century would also be good examples. It is significant that they were obliterated by state welfare in Germany and badly compromised by similar policy innovations (especially compulsory national insurance) in Britain. It is no coincidence that the idea of civil society developed in eastern Europe, where all forms of private associations were cruelly eliminated by the communist state. Under such circumstances no university could be independent.

However, perhaps a better description of the kind of social context in which independent universities flourish might be to draw upon Michael Oakeshott's[1] distinction between the state as an *enterprise association* and as a *civil association*. The trouble with civil society is that it has been used by the left as an anti-capitalist idea; indeed, many civil-society-type organisations have become agents of the state (especially in welfare), and the modern institutional progeny of civil society, the Non-Governmental Organisations, are fierce opponents of capitalism and globalisation. Oakeshott's distinction refers to organisations with a specific purpose, like a government department with a legitimate function or

---

1   See Michael Oakeshott (1975), *On Human Conduct*, Oxford University Press, Oxford.

a firm, and, in contrast, to a form of association with no specific purpose. The latter develops its own goals, outside any national 'plan', in an atmosphere of freedom. In the modern world the error has been to conceive of a whole range of human activities as if they could be organised under the rubric of a national project with specific targets. This style of politics actually operates outside communist states, especially in welfare, and was (and still is) a feature of conservative politics as much as socialist.

It is obvious that, in the enterprise state, universities will be made to serve a national purpose, to provide skilled manpower or even to advance some collective goal such as the country's status and prestige in the worlds of science and the humanities. What is clear is that in such a world universities will lack any serious kind of *autonomy*. The formal right of free speech or inquiry will be of little use if those who exercise it are denied the opportunity of acquiring financial independence and of holding independent property. Some of the critics of market-based higher education argued that universities have reduced autonomy to the extent that they depend on commercial sponsorship of research and market funding of staff salaries. But a much more decisive loss of autonomy occurs if they are expected to maintain government targets, for example in the promotion of certain academic subjects, while remaining formally free and independent. The great ancient European universities, Oxford, Cambridge and Paris, were not commercial organisations, but they were certainly autonomous. Indeed, the University of Salamanca in Spain promoted the idea of the free market in sixteenth-century Spain, against some of the teachings of the Catholic Church.

Is it possible for universities to remain autonomous in the sense described above in the absence of proper financial independence? If the state is the paymaster will it not ultimately determine the ends and purposes of universities? It is, of course, true that Oxford and Cambridge have been regulated by the state since the nineteenth century (indeed, they had fallen into disrepute precisely because they were not properly disciplined by competition), but they retained financial autonomy until the 20th century. Curiously, though, there is an example in British history in which almost complete state financial control did not lead to a loss of freedom and academic independence. I refer to the era of the University Grants Committee (UGC), founded in 1919, in which the state dispensed funds for nominally independent institutions yet took no part in the setting of targets and in the research and teaching interests of particular universities. It is true that there was a good deal of waste, incompetence and rent-seeking. Indeed, in the 1960s and 1970s the universities, so far from producing a public good, which the market allegedly could not provide, were generating a lot of negative externalities in the form of student unrest and dissident staff members. There were a lot of complaints about 'accountability', but that just illustrates the point about autonomy, for a truly autonomous body is not answerable to any outside authority, especially a democratically elected one. If it is to be so accountable it is bound to become the servant of politicians.

But despite inauspicious circumstances, the universities under the UGC did preserve considerable autonomy. As Kedourie said, they functioned 'like academic republics – the only genuine republics to subsist in the modern world – well-run, efficient and economic in their use of comparatively modern resources'.[2]

---

2   Elie Kedourie (1989), *Diamonds into Glass*, Centre for Policy Studies, London, p. 18.

But this could not last. Ever since Lord Robbins[3] had said in 1963 that in a democratic society there should be free education for everyone qualified to take advantage of it, there had been growing demands to expand the system. This has been more or less achieved, for now over one-third of those in the appropriate age cohort are in receipt of degree-level education (up from less than 10 per cent 30 years ago). But this improvement has been bought at a high cost. Not just in terms of the quality of the product being offered – and there are constant complaints that in the newer universities there has been almost a tangible decline in standards – but equally importantly in the nature of the universities themselves. The expansion has been accompanied by an inexorable increase in government control and a loss of genuine autonomy.

This process, which has been going on since the 1980s under both Conservative and Labour governments, has brought about the death knell of academic freedom. And this has come about through a complete misunderstanding of the notion of freedom in economic society. Successive governments have accurately identified an important feature of economic liberty – it leads to an efficient allocation of economic resources in society from which everybody benefits. If universities were free to raise their own money, charge their fees and fix their own salaries, they could fulfil this economic function by providing qualified personnel for a modern economy. But they could also pursue their traditional roles, for example pursuing research that had no obvious utilitarian value and sustaining cultural values that might be lost if the world were governed only by the price mechanism. That has been

3   Committee on Higher Education (1963), *Higher Education: Report* (the 'Robbins Report'), HMSO, Cmnd 2154, London. This became the 'bible' of educational progressives.

a feature of universities throughout their history. But since the 1980s they have been seen by governments exclusively in the crudest of economic terms, their existence justified only by how much they can contribute to national output. The UGC was ultimately closed down, to be replaced by the Higher Education Funding Council, a body which was explicitly charged with the requirement of providing teaching and research to meet the needs of society.

But even the promoters of this kind of utilitarian educational philosophy were ignorant of the economic philosophy from which it allegedly derived. For this specifically maintains that it is impossible for any centralised body to have the kind of knowledge which would enable it to predict accurately how many engineers, accountants and lawyers would be needed in, say, two years' time, or how many degree programmes in physics or chemistry would be required for an advanced industrial economy. This kind of knowledge (much of it 'tacit'[4]) is hidden in the interstices of a society and is not immediately available to planners. The state cannot mimic the free market in education any more than it can do so in the production of cars, clothes or food.

However, since the mid-1980s universities have been burdened with a plethora of demands from government, ranging from promoting socially needed courses to closing down some 'unfashionable' departments (for example, philosophy). Their funding depends on how successfully they meet centrally determined research criteria, and they have been blitzed with a mass of paperwork designed to increase 'efficiency'. But in a sense the universities only have themselves to blame for their loss of freedom.

---

4   See F. A. Hayek (1960), *The Constitution of Liberty*, Routledge and Kegan Paul, London, Part 1.

For they have resisted all attempts at privatisation, and only a few academics have shown any interest in charging full-cost fees. It is very difficult for private bodies to compete with a massively subsidised state system: the nominal £1,000 tuition charge, itself subject to means testing, is a derisory response to the demands of market economics in higher education.

The place of the state

It is clear that the state rationale for higher education is in some disarray. Even those traditionally most favourable to a state monopoly, academics themselves (especially the least competent), are beginning to protest at its inhibitions. It is surprising that those most enthusiastic about efficiency in higher education should have resisted an obvious method for improving the quality of academics, a competitive market in salaries. But the quasi-egalitarian pay structure persists so that personnel proceed dutifully up the salary scale with only a bold move to a new institution, or a leap over the grades, bringing some kind of reward for achievement. Once again it is the mediocre who gain.

A popular rationale for continued state involvement is now looking completely inadequate. It is the claim that a fully private system would be inequitable with educational opportunities limited to those who could afford the fees. But the state system has inequities of its own. The more or less zero-priced system is taken up disproportionately by the better off.[5] For the rich it is a very good system; the opportunity cost is very low since they do not require the wages of teenagers for the family budget and their educated

---

5   See Julian Le Grand (1982), *The Strategy of Equality*, Allen and Unwin, London.

children are assured of a good job when they leave university. Improvements have been made with the replacement of the maintenance grant by the loan system but the vast subsidy to fees remains. It is the better off who have benefited most from the expansion of higher education in the past few years.

It is also difficult to see what is left of the public-good argument for state involvement in higher education. This is the claim that universities provide benefits to society at large without being properly reimbursed for their cost. In a pure market society, therefore, these benefits would not be supplied and everybody would be worse off. Unprofitable scientific research might be an example, as would work in the humanities. The state has to step in to fill the gap. I have already suggested that the externalities of higher education were largely negative, with some staff members openly hostile to the society in which we live and largely occupied in whipping up dissent in the student body. This activity is no longer prevalent in universities; students themselves seem particularly immune to the political blandishments that used to be so popular. They are more concerned with getting a good job and unwittingly fulfilling a genuine utilitarian function of education. But there is little evidence that higher education provides some public good in the way of preserving a cultural tradition. Whether such a thing survives depends on a congeries of factors of which a thriving higher education system is only one. Certainly private universities provided some positive externalities a long time before the state got involved.

The demands for some privatisation of university education are so compelling that the only serious question might be about the particular form this should take. In what follows I certainly do not wish to pre-empt the case for any reform; whatever emerges spontaneously once the state has withdrawn is likely to be accept-able on both efficiency and moral grounds. However, what I want to discuss briefly are two rival forms of private university educa-tion – the pure market system, where price determines almost everything, and a voluntary arrangement where, outside the state, certain bodies emerge which supply a wanted service without being motivated by profit. This is the traditional private university and, although it has always enjoyed certain tax advantages, it is not in receipt of public funding. Also, its autonomy is guaranteed because it is not dependent on commercial sponsorship. For ex-ample, scientists are free to pursue their intellectual interests rather than research in areas which will generate profit. Milton Friedman[6] argues that such institutions are attractive to donors precisely because they are not governed by the profit motive: they appeal to our altruistic sentiments. However, he is quick to point out that private universities in America have better completion rates than state ones because they are offering a service to students who are in turn willing to pay for it.

However, historically there have been grave problems with this type of funding. Adam Smith, in *The Wealth of Nations*,[7] com-mented very critically on his experience at Oxford. The dons were incurably indolent, they did little research and had no time for the students. They lived off endowments. He went so far as to suggest that students should pay for their instruction directly at the class-room door so that those dons who could not attract any students would not earn any income. He was right, for this is the only way

---

6   Milton and Rose Friedman (1980), *Free to Choose,* Secker and Warburg, London, p. 177.

7   Adam Smith (1970), *The Wealth of Nations,* University of Chicago Press, Chicago, vol. 2, p. 283. First published 1776.

to produce an identity of interest between teacher and student. Jeremy Bentham made similar observations about Oxford just a few years after Smith. Indeed, it was the poor performance of Oxford and Cambridge which led to their public regulation in the nineteenth century.

The problem with all universities that depend heavily on endowments is that the donor has no control over his funds once he has given them away. They become the property of the faculty to spend as they wish. This is as true today as it was of the eighteenth century. The rise of some dubious academic disciplines in the highly endowed American system is a subject of some concern. It is significant that political correctness and limitations on free speech have been a major feature of private universities in America. Could commerce do any better?

I must confess to being a victim of the anti-commercial way of thinking myself. In 1994 I wrote that if universities were 'marketed like public companies, concerned solely with returns to owners, they would provide almost exclusively vocational education and their research would be limited to that financed by private industry. It is easy to see how such an arrangement would be inconsistent with the idea of civil society.'[8] But this is a form of nirvana economics. Of course, in an ideal world universities would be free from commercial constraint and could pursue pure research without thought of cost. But in the real world we have to make comparisons between necessarily imperfect arrangements, and it is by no means the case that the conventional system of private universities that exists in America, and which is recommended for

---

8   See Norman Barry (1994), *The Case for Independent Universities*, Buckingham University Press, Buckingham, p. 13.

Britain, is the most effective mechanism for realising the ideals of higher education.

As some important research by James Tooley[9] has revealed, there is a 'global' educational industry in which private institutions, often for profit, provide a wanted service according to supply and demand. Consumer choice determines what is offered and high standards are maintained without supervision by the state. It is noticeable that these new universities emerged often in response to perceived inadequacies of the state system. At the moment the main examples are non-European, primarily in South America and in parts of the 'third world'. The most successful are in Brazil, Argentina and in India, where NIIT provides a superbly efficient computer educational service with 400 campuses, a market share of 37 per cent, annual turnover of $73 million and profits of $13 million (1999 figures). It provides a qualification with international recognition. The institutions described by Tooley provide freedom for learning and the pursuit of knowledge with few of the features of traditional, voluntary non-market bodies. It is the presence of the profit motive which prevents their capture by self-interested faculty. Some of the conventional disadvantages of private education, such as consumer ignorance and asymmetric information between ill-informed purchasers and adroit suppliers of the service in search of a quick profit, are easily overcome. The suppliers establish 'brand names' which guarantee reliability, and the market has proved its fecundity in creating mechanisms for monitoring the service for quality. Some of the private universities studied by Tooley have generated pure research. Bilkent

---

9   See James Tooley (1999), *The Global Education Industry,* Institute of Economic Affairs, London.

University in Turkey, which is private but not for-profit, has managed to attract scholars of international reputation. It would continue to do so if it were allowed to be fully private and profit-making.

What is also important is that Tooley shows that many of the traditional features of private universities are not only not necessary but may also not be quality inducing. A good example is endowments, which 'can undermine a company's incentives to innovate and work efficiently'.[10] Again, with regard to the equity question, if one makes a comparison between the confirmed inequities of the state system in the provision of higher education and the market, it is by no means the case that the private, profit-driven world is more inegalitarian; that it caters only for an élite. As Tooley shows,[11] private companies have responded to the needs of the disadvantaged and introduced programmes of effective social responsibility. As history demonstrates, the poor have always been anxious to extend opportunities to their children at all levels of education. The expansion of private provision provides just those opportunities which had been denied to previous generations.

Conclusion

A free society will provide a variety of educational opportunities. That is the essence of pluralism. The manifest deficiency of the state university system has heightened interest in alternative provision, but it is wrong to suppose that there are only two possibili-

---

10   Ibid, p. 28.
11   Ibid, ch. 5.

ties – the state monopoly and the traditional voluntary, non-profit bodies. Both types have problems: opportunism and rent-seeking by staff, lack of response to student demand and, in the state system especially, perverse redistribution to the better off.

What is required if pluralism is to be activated in Britain is a change in the fee structure so that the existing state-dominated system is open to competition. At present we have only one fully privately funded university, Buckingham, which fulfils some of the functions of a traditional university. There are private bodies of a mainly vocational kind. But all these institutions are hampered by the fact that they have to charge economic fees, while the government-funded institutions do not. If there were a genuine 'level playing field' a variety could emerge and easily offer a range of courses which would not only meet the labour needs of a complex industrial society but would also satisfy the traditional demands of higher education, such as the pursuit of pure research and the preservation of a cultural tradition. It is only the state's quasi-monopoly and the stultifying presence of other privileges which prevent this happening.

12 BACK TO THE FUTURE
Terence Kealey

The modern Western university originated in the market in medieval Italy. Greek scholars including Plato, Aristotle and Pythagoras had earlier, of course, created institutions of higher learning, scholarship and research – and related institutions including the Library in Alexandria had survived into Hellenistic times – but the collapse of the Roman Empire took the extant institutions of study down with it.

During the Dark Ages (now sometimes known as the Early Middle Ages), certain European monarchs and churchmen including Charlemagne and Alcuin of York helped revive learning through the creation of cathedral and secular schools. The Arabs, too, studied the Hellenistic texts they inherited and the Indian scholarship they encountered; but the modern Western university did not emerge until market forces conceived it, in Italy.

The market, though, had first to emerge. The late Roman Empire, which had degenerated into a military dictatorship commanding a centralised economy, had crushed much of its own commerce, and the chaos of the Dark Ages had destroyed most of the residual trade in Europe; yet trade was never completely extinguished in Italy, whose social and commercial infrastructures proved surprisingly robust in the face of the barbarian invasions (in contrast, trade was almost completely extinguished in Britain, where coins disappeared – coins continued to be minted in Italy throughout the Dark Ages).

Moreover, during the late 700s a 70-year truce was negotiated between the Christians of southern Italy and the Arabs of northern Africa. With peace secured, the old imperial trade in timber, dried fruits, linen, wine, cheese and manufactured articles, including desks, bedspreads, pillows and embroidered silk between southern Italy, Sicily and north Africa, was revived. Subsequently, Italian commerce grew and spread, with merchants from Venice, Pisa, Florence and Genoa regularly visiting Damascus, Alexandria and other eastern entrepôts.

Straddling the trading crossroads between the Mediterranean and northern Europe, Italy was well placed to pioneer Europe's Commercial Revolution. Consequently, it was Italy where the instruments of commerce were honed. As Professor Einzig showed in his *History of Foreign Exchange*,[1] the first known foreign exchange contract was issued in Genoa in 1156 to allow two brothers who had borrowed 115 Genoese pounds to reimburse the bank's agents in Constantinople with 460 bezants within a month of their arrival; and it was Italy that invented cheques (the first was written in Pisa during the fourteenth century), bills of exchange (effectively postdated cheques) and deposit banking. By the twelfth century the Italians had invented the modern or 'premium' variety of insurance, the Florentines had transformed accountancy by inventing double-entry bookkeeping; and in 1412 they awarded the world's first patent (from *patere*, the Latin for 'lie open', as in 'patently obvious').

And it was Italy that created the first great banks. The Florentine Medici bank, in the time of Cosimo (1399–1464), had

---

1 Paul Einzig, *The History of Foreign Exchange*, London, 1971.

branches in Rome, Milan, Pisa, Venice, Avignon, Geneva, Bruges and London. Indeed, the very word 'bank' comes from the Italian *banca*, meaning 'bench', because the early bankers sat on benches at the side of the markets; if a banker failed, his bench was ceremonially broken, so we get 'bankrupt' from *ruptus*, the Latin for break.

As Italy pioneered the rebirth of commerce, so it created the *lex mercatoria*, the Law Merchant, which was the body of commercial law generated and enforced by the merchants themselves (see Bruce Benson's *Enterprise of Law* for a historical account[2]). But the generation of the Law Merchant created a demand for professional lawyers to draft, negotiate and police contracts under the Law. In 1050 a group of young men in Bologna collected together in a college (from *collegium*, the Latin for a society or company) to recruit experienced practitioners to teach them. So, nearly a thousand years ago, the first modern university in Europe was created – as a law school founded, funded and directed by its students. Traces of this customer initiative linger in the tradition (still maintained in Scotland as well as in some of the older Italian universities) of the Rector (the highest officer in the institution, who corresponds to an English chancellor) being elected by the student body.

And Italy fostered the rebirth of science. Consider mathematics. The Indians and Arabs had invented decimal numerals which, in 1202, Leonardo Fibonacci of Pisa transmitted to Europe in his *Liber Abaci*; but the Italians then innovated. The ancients had solved linear and quadratic equations, but in the intervening centuries there had been no advance in solving cubic equations until,

---

2   Bruce Benson, *The Enterprise of Law*, San Francisco, 1990.

in 1510, Scipione del Ferro discovered the solution to the cubic equation of the form $x^3 + mx + n = 0$, where there is no simple x term. In 1534 Niccolò Tartaglia found the solution to the cubic equation $x^3 + px^2 = n$, where there is no simple x term, and in 1545 Gerolamo Cardono published his *Ars magna*, the major mathematics book of the era, which incorporated the solution to the quartic equation discovered by his own servant, Lodovico Ferrari.

These mathematical discoveries were financed by the market. Tartaglia, who worked in Venice, was a freelance maths teacher, and there were many of those and many small private maths schools or *scuolae d'abbaco* (as in 'abacus') in Italy at the time; they were the MBA professors and business schools of their day. They taught the basic arithmetic, algebraic, geometric, accountancy and navigational skills of the market to an increasingly commercial and long-distance trading society; and Italian boys hoping to do business had to attend them.

To raise their profiles, and their fees, the private mathematicians including Tartaglia competed to publish original research – just as academics still do. Thus we see that the Western custom of publishing novel research grew out of the Italian market in academic institutions (previously, novel research had generally been kept secret by its inventors, and that confidentiality is still maintained today by for-profit organisations: it was the Italian academic market that created the contemporary public paradigm).

In time, the established universities expanded to compete with the *scuolae d'abbaco*: Del Ferro himself taught at the University of Bologna, no less, which competed with the *scuolae* for the students' fees. And Italy inaugurated another Western tradition, that of the private endowment of academic institutions. Cardono taught in Milan at the Piattine schools, which had been founded by a bequest of Tommaso Piatti. Italy even pioneered an early sexual equality, for many of Bologna's professors, when it was still a predominantly market-led institution, were female.

Thus we see that the modern Western university, with many of its most cherished attributes, emerged out of the commerce of Italy, to serve that commerce. And thus we also see that Buckingham's contemporary structure, as a market-led institution focusing on the teaching of law and business, mirrors that of the earliest Western universities.

But the religious and secular authorities of medieval Europe feared the universities, and the Church soon acquired control over them, as is witnessed by their vocabulary, terms such as 'chancellor', 'bachelor' or 'doctor' being ecclesiastical imports. And, as the Church tightened its grip on the universities, so they ceased to function usefully. Sometimes this was because the Church simply oppressed academics. So, for example, Cardono, the greatest mathematician of medieval Europe, was imprisoned by the Inquisition for casting the horoscope of Jesus Christ, an episode he described in his autobiographical *Book of my Life*.

Other episodes of oppression are legion: but more invidiously the Church learned to pre-empt the need by simply taking over the universities and nipping any heterodoxy in the bud. The contrast between the academic freedoms of the twelfth century – when an almost modern and liberal world seems about to dawn – and the oppressions and repressions of the thirteenth, is well described by Hugh Trevor Roper in his 1989 book *The Rise of Christian Europe*. Consider eighteenth-century Oxford. Other contributors to this book have quoted Gibbon's and Smith's denunciations of the Oxford of the day; let me just note that an institution whose teachers' primary qualification was that they were unmarried priests of the

Church of England who subscribed to the Thirty Nine Articles, whose teachers' average age was 23, and whose teachers' usual ambition was to leave for a parochial living carrying the right to marry, was hardly likely to carry the torch of learning very high.

But, to quote Margaret Thatcher, 'You can't buck the market', and as the universities declined into irrelevance so other institutions in England (and let me now focus on England) arose to meet society's needs for scholarship, education, research and qualifications. Thus the Royal Society emerged in 1662 from the unofficial 'Invisible College' of researchers that had gathered discreetly over the previous decades, while the Inns of Court and the various Royal Colleges of medicine assumed ever greater responsibilities for secular professional education and qualifications.

Later, as the Agricultural and Industrial Revolutions accelerated, so informal research societies like the Lunatics of Birmingham (so called because its members met on the nights of the full moon to ease their return home by night) arose, as did a plethora of provincial Literary and Philosophical Societies (the one in Newcastle-upon-Tyne is among those that still flourish). Professional, privately funded but non-university research institutions also emerged: these included the Pneumatic Institute in Clifton (where in 1798 Humphry Davy discovered the anaesthetic properties of nitrous oxide or laughing gas) and the Royal Institution (where in 1831 Michael Faraday discovered electromagnetic induction). Meanwhile, privately funded vocational training flourished, with no fewer than 700 Mechanics' Institutes being founded between 1820 and 1850 alone.

During this time of ferment and of British industrial leadership, Oxford and Cambridge slumbered, but eventually new universities were created privately to provide the education and research that industry demanded. Typical was Mason College, later Birmingham University, endowed by Josiah Mason, a successful local industrialist. On laying the foundation stone in 1875 he said: 'I, who have never been blessed with children of my own, may yet, in these students, leave behind me an intelligent, earnest, industrious and truth-loving and truth-seeking progeny for generations to come.'[3]

The new universities included London (1836), Manchester (1851), Newcastle-upon-Tyne (1852), Birmingham (1900), Liverpool (1903), Leeds (1904) and Sheffield (1905). (Those are the dates of the Royal Charters; the universities originated in older privately founded colleges which only received their charters after they had established their reputations. No fewer than eleven university colleges were founded privately in England between 1851 and 1892.) Finally, after the passage of the 1870 Education Act (the 'Forster Act'), Oxford and Cambridge rejoined secular society as functioning universities rather than as theological training schools of celibates who dabbled in some non-theological subjects.

But Oxford and Cambridge did bequeath to the newer universities their custom (which originated in the parson's freehold of the Church of England) that academics should have tenure, which, for all its potential for abuse, did at least embody the concept that universities should be free to pursue knowledge on their own terms, not on anyone else's. The advance of knowledge is a Darwinian affair: it cannot be preordained, it is best achieved if a thousand flowers bloom, and if selection is then made between those ideas. Most of those flowers will be weeds requiring rigorous selection, but if the thousand flowers are not allowed first to bloom,

3   Quoted in R. O. Berdahl, *British Universities and the State*, Cambridge, 1959.

then no new ideas will emerge between which selection can be made.

Yet the universities, sadly, have brought forth too few flowers. The unfortunate truth is that the intellectual history of Europe since the fall of the Roman Empire has been driven more by ideas generated outside the universities rather than those generated within them. The universities have been, only too often, bastions of sterility, reaction and even of cruelty.

But the universities have rarely been free; where they have been, as were the new English universities of the nineteenth century, then the names we associate with them (particularly with London – Bentham's mummified corpse still stands guard over University College London) speak of the great benefits society accrued from that freedom. In the US today the independent universities are free, and they are the unacknowledged legislators of the world, generating the economic and social ideas that dominate our globalised planet.

But a university's freedom is built in part on an assured income. The new English universities were free, in part, because the nineteenth century was an era of remarkable growth and of constant prices. The universities could thus grow steadily, confident in their ever-rising rolls (driven by the needs and dividends of a self-enriching society) and in the returns on their investments.

It was war which destroyed the universities' autonomy. In particular, it was World War I, whose inflation reduced the value of the universities' fixed-income investments by 75 per cent and whose needs for manpower reduced their recruitment income by a similar figure. By 1918 the universities collectively were threatened with bankruptcy. They turned to the government for help; 1914–18 marks the end of university autonomy in the UK.

The government had for some time supported the universities in a small way. Indeed, the Scottish government had long supported the universities north of the border, and after the Union of 1707 these commitments were continued, amounting to £5,077 in 1832, for example. The English and Welsh universities, however, were self-supporting, though they did receive payments from the government for particular services: in 1841, for example, London University received £3,320 for its role as the central examination body for the colonies.

But when, in 1872 for example, the Welsh University Colleges asked for support, they were told 'it had never been [government] policy to give financial assistance for the promotion of higher education in England'.[4] Eventually, though, grants had to be made in Wales (£4,000 to Aberystwyth in 1882, and similar sums to Cardiff in 1883 and Bangor in 1884) because those colleges were close to bankruptcy.

Subsequently, the English university colleges united to press for government money. The academics were not so much jealous of their Welsh as of their German counterparts, who luxuriated in vast government subventions. On 9 May 1887 representatives of the colleges met in Southampton to co-ordinate their campaign, and for the rest of the year they bombarded the press. On 21 March 1887, for example, Thomas Huxley wrote in *The Times*: 'We have already entered upon the most serious struggle for existence to which this country has ever been committed. The latter years of the century promise to see us in an industrial war of far more serious import than the military wars of its opening years.' On 1 July 1887, Sir John Lubbock wrote in *The Times*: 'The claims of these col-

---

4   Ibid.

leges were not based alone on their service to learning and study; they were calculated to contribute largely to the material prospect of the country.'

Lord Salisbury was persuaded, and in 1889 an *ad hoc* Committee on Grants to University Colleges was given £15,000 to dispense between eleven colleges. By 1903, fourteen colleges were sharing £27,000 annually between them. But these were small sums: no college received more than £2,000, yet as early as 1872 Birmingham, for example, had a total budget of £13,089, of which about half came from fees, and half from endowments.

In 1904, the Committee was given £54,000 to spend annually, £100,000 in 1905 and £150,000 in 1912, but these sums still only accounted for some 10–20 per cent of the civic universities' income; and Oxford and Cambridge stayed aloof, glorying in their total independence. Before 1914 Oxford and Cambridge had distrusted government intervention, and they despised the Germans for their technocratic, utilitarian, qualification-obsessed universities. A well-known nineteenth-century Oxford ditty went:

Professors we, from over the sea,
From the land where Professors in plenty be,
And we thrive and flourish, as well as may,
In the land that produced one Kant with a K,
And many Cants with a C.

But by 1918 Oxford and Cambridge joined the Universities' Deputation to the Treasury, petitioning the government for money. In the words of its leader, Sir Oliver Lodge, Principal of Birmingham University: 'It is suggested that we might ask for a doubling of the grant now and a doubling soon. But reconstruction is in the air, demobilisation is upon us; we cannot wait; we want these two doublings put together, we want a quadrupling at once. This is what we ask for.'

He got it. In 1919, the Universities Grants Committee was instituted, with a budget of over £1 million. This was not a single gift, designed to help the universities through the postwar period until they could resume an autonomous existence; this was annual, constitutive intervention on the German model. By 1921 the UGC's grant was £1,840,832 per annum. In 1936 it was £2,100,000 per annum.

Thus were the universities effectively nationalised. In 1914, only some 20 per cent of their income had come from the state, but by 1921, when local education authority grants were included, more than 50 per cent of the universities' income came from government bodies. This proportion continued to rise because, after 1919, private donations to the universities dried up. The universities were increasingly understood to be a government responsibility, and, moreover, potential donors were hard hit by the new postwar taxes, the government's share of GDP rising from around 10 per cent before 1914 to around 25 per cent in 1919 (and around 45 per cent after 1945).

In 1945 the annual UGC grant was doubled from £2,149,000 per annum to £4,149,000; it stood at £9,000,000 in 1947 and £15,000,000 in 1952. In 1953, under the Tories, it jumped to £20,000,000, and by 1957 was £25,000,000. The numbers of academics kept on doubling, from 5,000 in 1938/39 to 11,000 in 1954/55. Then, in 1958, a UGC minute initiated the universities of East Anglia (1963), Essex (1964), Kent (1965), Lancaster (1964), Sussex (1961), Warwick (1965) and York (1963). By 1961 the UGC was spending £39,500,000 a year in recurrent grants, as well as spending £12,000,000 a year on capital expansion, and by 1962 the numbers of academics had risen to 15,682. The Robbins Report was published in 1963, spawning a further fourteen universities, and by 1967 the numbers of academics had risen to 25,839, to achieve 32,738 in 1976. The numbers of students rose *pro rata*.

The arguments that academics and governments used to justify this vast state funding of higher education were all adumbrated by Sir Oliver Lodge in 1918 on behalf of the universities' deputation to the Treasury. So, for example, he claimed that Germany's economic performance had been attributed to the fact that 'The German universities are sustained by a State Grant averaging 72 per cent of their total income'.

But that was a false argument: the American government supported no universities (except for some agricultural colleges), yet the American economy was outstripping both Germany's and Britain's. Contrary to myth, the German economy did not overtake the UK's until after 1945 when, paradoxically, it was refashioned in the British image by the occupying powers. Between 1830 and 1939, German GDP per capita remained at two-thirds that of the UK.[5] It was the US whose GDP per capita converged on the UK's, overtaking it around 1890 – and that was under a regime of educational *laissez-faire*.

But academics (and politicians anxious, under the doctrine of public choice theory, to find legitimate areas to support and govern) will always find 'another country' which is apparently prospering thanks to the government funding of the universities. During the 1950s and 1960s it was, incredibly, the USSR.

On 10 January 1956, Harold Wilson wrote in the *Daily Mirror* that: 'In the next generation Russia's industrial challenge may well

5   Angus Maddison, *Phases of Capitalist Development*, Oxford, 1982.

dominate the world economic scene.' Nye Bevan told the Labour Conference that the world's economic leader would soon be the USSR: 'The challenge is going to come from Russia, not from the United States, West Germany nor from France. The challenge is going to come from those countries who ... are able to reap the material fruits of economic planning. In a modern complex society it is impossible to get national order by leaving things to private economic adventure.'

The USSR's *Sputnik* was launched in 1957, and this 'success' confirmed that the Soviet system of state universities and state science was the way forward. In his 1959 essay *The Two Cultures*, C. P. Snow wrote that: 'The Russians have a deeper insight into the scientific revolution than anyone else.' And the 1963 Robbins Report quoted with approval the Russian official who explained that the USSR's economic supremacy, based on vast education in science, was inevitable because 'the Soviet Union would always have use for people who had been trained to the limit of their potential ability'.

In 1963 Wilson delivered his famous 'White Heat of Technological Revolution' speech to the party conference at Scarborough, where he said that he would expand the universities because 'Those of us who have studied the formidable Soviet challenge in the education of scientists and technologists ... know where our future lies ... ' Thomas Balogh, the Balliol economist who advised Wilson, wrote: 'Russian output per head will surpass that of Britain in the early 1960s and that of the US in the mid-1970s.'

The Robbins Report was implemented, generously. So profoundly did Britain adopt the government funding of higher education and of science as its totems that in his 1964 *Inadmissible Evidence* John Osborne could create a heroic character, Bill Maitland, whose only faith was 'in the technological revolution, the pressing, growing pressing, urgent need for more and more scientists, and more scientists, for more and more schools and universities and universities and schools, the theme of change, realistic decisions based on a highly developed and professional study of society by people who really know their subject, the overdue need for us to adapt ourselves to different conditions . . . '

And what was the result of all this government-funded science, technology and higher education? Economic disaster. So comprehensively did the policy fail that, in September 1976, the Labour government had to hand over the management of the economy to the International Monetary Fund in return for a vast loan. Britain had joined the ranks of the Third World, as would soon the USSR itself. So bad was Britain's economic performance after 1964, and so disillusioned with higher education and science did the politicians become, that in 1971 Mrs Shirley Williams, who had been Labour's Secretary of State for Education and Science, warned that 'for the scientists the party is over'. By then, British universities enjoyed the highest staff–student ratios in the world, so during the 1980s these were allowed to slip to US levels, and despite all the fuss it was only then that the UK economy finally took off again.

But the real danger in government funding of universities does not lie in their economic failure but in their submission to the ideologies of the state. Witness the German universities. As Mark Walker showed in his *Science, Medicine and Cultural Imperialism*,[6] the German universities have a shameful record. They supported the nationalist imperialism of Bismarck and the Kaiser, but they actively distanced themselves from the democratic struggles of the

---

6   Mark Walker, *Science, Medicine and Cultural Imperialism*, New York, 1991.

Weimar Republic, only to support the nationalism, aggression and racism of Hitler.

Indeed, the German universities' support for Hitler was extraordinary. As the historian G. W. Craig noted, by 1933 'the great majority of the holders of university chairs' in Germany had joined the Nazi Party, long before they had needed to.[7] In his *Rektoral* address at the University of Freiburg, Martin Heidegger, the philosopher, called on his colleagues to recognise Adolf Hitler as the leader whom destiny had called upon to save the nation. In another *Rektoral* address in Regensburg, Professor Gotz Freiher von Polnitz proclaimed the accession of Hitler as the 'hour of victory'. In Tübingen the professor of Volkskunder (folkloric studies), Gustav Bebermeyer, announced, 'Now the great wonder has occurred. The German people has arisen!' The German universities had been so corrupted by their dependence on government that in 1945 over 4,000 academics had to be dismissed for active Nazism; several thousand further members of the party were allowed to retain their positions.

But the German universities were little better in 1914. One of the first victims of Germany's invasion of Belgium in August 1914 was the library of the University of Louvain (founded in 1425). The burning of the library consumed 300,000 books and over a thousand medieval and original manuscripts. The world was shocked, so Adolf von Harnack, the doyen of German theology, gathered together 92 of the most distinguished German academics to distribute a justification of the burning of the library, and the invasion of Belgium, on the grounds that international scholarship should only survive if it supported German foreign policy because, even in

---

7   G. W. Craig, *The Germans*, London, 1991.

1914, that policy was dedicated to preserving the integrity of the white race.

In 1915, 352 of the country's most prominent professors, including Ulrich von Wilamowitz-Moellendorf, Eduard Meyer, Otto von Gierke and Adolf Wagner, signed the Declaration of Intellectuals, which announced that it would be reasonable and just for Germany to acquire Belgium, France's channel coast and all of its important mineral areas, Courland, the Ukraine, and extensive colonial territories as the price of peace. Because the German universities were created by the state and were funded almost exclusively by the state they have too rarely elevated the search for truth above *realpolitik*.

The British universities never fell so low, but perhaps only because they were never so pressurised. As John Murray, the Principal of Exeter University College, commented in 1935, when state funding for universities exceeded £2 million a year: 'A university is like a man, it may gain the whole world and lose its own soul.' The universities have certainly imperilled their souls by consistently claiming knowledge to be a 'public good' that the private sector would never supply. In Sir Oliver Lodge's words in 1918: 'The development and maintenance of the universities is a national duty because they are a national benefit.'

But if knowledge really were a public good then people would not need to attend universities; they could just acquire the knowledge at will. It is precisely because knowledge is so difficult to acquire that people need intensive assistance in its acquisition: knowledge is effectively a private good (it is close to a club good in its qualities[8]). But so keen have the academics been to receive government money, they

---

8   Terence Kealey and Omar Al-Ubaydli, 'Should Governments Fund Science?'; Omar Al-Ubaydli and Terence Kealey, 'Endogenous Growth Theory: a Critique'; *Economic Affairs*, 4–9, 10–13, 2000.

have sacrificed their proper concerns over autonomy.

And sacrifice they have. When in May 1946 the government's Barlow Committee on Scientific Manpower demanded that 'the State should increasingly concern itself with positive University policy', the Committee of Vice-Chancellors and Principals replied that 'they will be glad to have a greater measure of guidance from the Government'.

This has remained the pattern. When, on 23 March 1987, Sir George Porter, the President of the Royal Society, wrote in the *Independent* asking for more government money for science, he also asked for greater government control. He wrote: 'What Britain needs is a clear and visible long-term policy for the whole of science and technology, determined and accepted at the highest level: a policy which co-ordinates both science education and research, universities and industry. Many of us in this country believe that the Prime Minister should set up, and herself chair, a high-level National Science Council, to determine our overall science policy.'

It almost beggars belief to witness senior professors actually asking for their academic freedom to be removed. But the government money was 'dazzling', as John Murray wrote in 1947. As the Vice-Chancellor of Oxford complained in 1948, 'we are in danger of being killed by kindness'. And killed they nearly were. I have written elsewhere of how the 1980s campaign that the universities conducted (when they claimed to be in decline) was based on false statistics, as was Oxford University's justification for refusing Margaret Thatcher an honorary degree in 1985.[9]

And the British universities continue to collude in their own subservience. The University Grants Committee was originally

9   Terence Kealey, *The Economic Laws of Scientific Research*, London, 1996.

established under the Haldane Principle, named for the distinguished Liberal politician, which theoretically preserved academic freedom. Thus the UGC was largely made up of academics, whose funding came from the State but whose decisions were autonomous. But the UGC has now been supplanted by the Higher Education Funding Council for England (HEFCE), which is dominated by industrialists, not academics, and the universities accepted that supplanting with barely a whimper.

The public universities today are closely regulated by the state, one of whose creatures is the Quality Assurance Agency. This inspectorate is now so intrusive that, early in 2001, the academic board of the London School of Economics condemned it for having 'infringed academic freedom, imposed its own bureaucratic and pedagogical agenda, neglected student intellectual development, and used incompetent and unprofessional reviewers'.

How refreshing! Finally the universities are beginning to fight back; and indeed the government, surprised by the universities' reaction, has reined in the QAA. And how interesting that it should have been the LSE, one of the least government-dependent schools in the UK (many of the LSE's students come from abroad), which led the revolt, for academic and political autonomy flow out of economic autonomy.

The great universities in the world today are the American independents, including Harvard, Yale, Princeton, Chicago and Stanford. They are independent because, being privately endowed ($19.2 billion in the case of Harvard alone), they need not take government money for teaching and they are selective of the money they take for research. The importance of independence to academic quality is illustrated by the vast mass of European and Asian universities which, though heavily funded by their governments, fail to write, say or do anything of importance.

Even worse, a dependence on the state, even a democratic state, leads the universities, for fear of offending their funders, to censor their own activities. The most influential academic worldwide of recent decades, as judged by the political impact of his scholarship, has been Milton Friedman, but no publicly funded university could have fostered such an opponent of the state. That is why Friedman worked at Chicago.

Buckingham was created 25 years ago to provide the UK with an independent forum where ideas can be pursued fearlessly. Perhaps our greatest contribution to date has been the very fact of our existence – we bear witness to the fact that an independent university can survive in the UK, a fact that many doubted in 1976. But by maintaining staff–student ratios of 10:1 (double that of the university sector on average) we have shown how to maintain traditional standards and we have demonstrated how the government funding of the state's universities has simply displaced or 'crowded out' the private money that would otherwise be there. It is outrageous that the state refuses to allow its universities to charge top-up fees.

If we can find the endowments, we will one day challenge the great US benchmarks. We will hope to challenge them in terms of social equity, for like them we will seek to operate 'needs-blind' admissions policies, and we will hope to challenge them academically too. We were created by bold visionaries. Let us maintain their standards.

Acknowledgements

I thank Professor John Clarke for his useful comments.

The final section of this book reprints Professor Harry S. Ferns's pathbreaking paper, *Towards an Independent University*, published by the Institute of Economic Affairs at the beginning of 1969 as Occasional Paper 25.

As explained in the Editor's Introduction to Professor Ferns's paper, the Institute had been discussing the idea of an independent university since the summer of 1966 but it was the Ferns paper which began a '... discussion from first principles that (left) no assumption unexamined' and which resulted eventually in the establishment of the University of Buckingham.

The reprint which follows is of the first edition of the paper. A second edition was published in 1970 with a Postscript by Professor Ferns in which he discussed progress towards an independent university in the intervening year.

In the Introduction to this volume, Professor James Tooley explains the relevance of Professor Ferns's ideas to the present state of the universities.

13

TOWARDS AN INDEPENDENT UNIVERSITY

A View of the Urgent Need for Establishing an Institution of Higher Education Free from Government Control

H. S. FERNS

Professor of Political Science, University of Birmingham

CONTENTS

INSTITUTE OF ECONOMIC AFFAIRS: OCCASIONAL PAPERS

As part of its educational purpose in explaining the light that economists and others concerned with the optimum use of scarce resources can throw on policy in industry or government, the Institute is reprinting, as *Occasional Papers*, essays or addresses judged of interest to wider audiences than those to which they were originally directed.

Since its establishment in 1957 as a research and educational foundation wholly independent of governmental funds and influence, with its integrity assured by drawing finance from a wide diversity of sources, the directors of the Institute have been increasingly concerned with the independence of scholarship, learning and research in economics, and have invited economists concerned specifically with education to consider the implications of governmental and private financing. Several publications indicate their findings.

For some years the increasing financing of universities by government has provoked thought on the urgency of at least one major centre of university teaching and research that would be free of government finance and therefore of political influence. Such a project had been discussed among the Institute's officers and advisers, most specifically in the summer of 1966 with two distinguished economists teaching at a British and an American university. Ways and means were considered of starting an independent university on a small scale with finance from industry and students and teaching talent from economists and social scientists in other parts of the world anxious about the independence of universities.

Accordingly, when in the summer of 1967 Professor H. S. Ferns discussed the subject in the *Political Quarterly*,[1] the Institute invited him to elaborate his thinking in a *Paper* to be published by the Institute in order to stimulate thought among academics, educationists, public men and industrialists. While the *Paper* was being written, the interest of other academics was sought and received, and it was thought desirable to discuss a draft at a small conference in March 1968 and at a larger gathering in July 1968. Professor Ferns has taken into account some of the comments made at these meetings and subsequently, but his *Paper* remains substantially as it was originally written. It is now being published simultaneously with a third meeting on 8–9 January 1969 of academics and others to discuss the practical steps in establishing an independent university.

Professor Ferns' *Paper* can be left to speak for itself. It is an incisive, penetrating and constructive consideration of the reasons for and some of the problems of establishing an independent university in a country in which the notion has been uncritically accepted that education must be a function of government. Professor Ferns is rightly concerned at this stage only with arguing the general principle and with outlining a possible structure of organisation, teaching, research, and finance. Acceptance of the general objective must precede deliberation on detail.

The main obstacle to overcome may be the conventional as-

1   'A Radical Proposal for the Universities', *Political Quarterly*, July–September 1967.

sumption that only government can finance higher education. Not only politicians, but also businessmen and educationists have accepted and acted on this assumption; and students who resent university regulations have also acquiesced in the common fallacy. The truth is that all the finance for education that has been increasingly channelled through government is private in origin. Higher education is financed by private businessmen who pay company taxation and by individuals who pay income, purchase and capital taxes. There is no necessary reason why their moneys should be channelled to the universities indirectly through governments, so that universities are accountable to politicians, and not directly by consumers of university teachings and buyers of university services, so that the universities are answerable to them as customers.

This is the underlying truth that has long lain buried beneath layers of historical convenience and accident and which Professor Ferns uncovers in his scholarly, spirited and inspiriting *Paper*. It is in the long tradition of English liberalism of David Hume, Adam Smith and John Stuart Mill among the classics, echoed in our day by Professor Max Beloff, Professor Ernst Chain, Dr R. B. McCallum and other scholars of a wide range of social philosophy and political sympathy concerned about the deliberate influences of government on university scholarship. The Institute hopes it will begin a discussion from first principles that will leave no assumption unexamined and which will end before too long in the establishment of an independent university in Britain.

The *Paper* is followed by a declaration in support of the general principle of an independent university.

EDITOR

December 1968

THE AUTHOR

H. S. Ferns, MA, PhD (Cantab), is a Canadian who was educated at St John's High School, Winnipeg, the University of Manitoba, and Trinity College, Cambridge, where he secured a distinguished first class in the Historical Tripos and was elected Earl of Derby's Historical Scholar and a scholar of the Goldsmiths' Company. He has worked at Harvard University and the University of Chicago. During World War II he served on the secretarial staff of the Rt Hon. W. Mackenzie King, Prime Minister of Canada. While teaching in Canada between 1945 and 1949 he founded a co-operatively owned daily newspaper and served as a conciliation officer in the Department of Labour of the Government of Manitoba. Since 1950 he has been successively Senior Lecturer, Head of Department and Professor of Political Science at the University of Birmingham. For four years (1961–5) he served as Dean of the Faculty of Commerce and Social Science and was a Member of the Council of the University of Birmingham. He is a member of the Executive Committee of the Sparkbrook Association, Birmingham, which is concerned with problems of urban renewal and racial integration.

Professor Ferns' publications include *Britain and Argentina in the Nineteenth Century* (Oxford University Press, 1960) and *The Age of Mackenzie King: The Rise of the Leader* (Heinemann, 1955).

TOWARDS AN INDEPENDENT UNIVERSITY

The case

There are four principal reasons why an independent university should be established now.

Independence

The first reason is moral and social. For nearly three-quarters of a century more and more people of all classes and occupations have become more and more dependent in one way or another upon the state and have accordingly come under its control. It is now becoming increasingly obvious that this dependence and control are doing the community more harm than good, and that the moral and social energy of the people is diminishing through undue and prolonged entanglements in the web of government. The time has come to demonstrate on a large scale and in a sophisticated sphere of human endeavour and necessity that people on their own can meet a community need with no assistance from the state and entirely without state controls other than those designed to preserve the common law rights of individuals. To this end it is here proposed that an independent university be established for the provision of general higher education, the advancement of knowledge and the inculcation of habits of mental and moral discipline.

Such an act of initiative and free co-operation among individuals will energise the community as a whole and serve to kindle the enthusiasm and focus the hope of all who are unwilling to believe that the fate of Britain is to become a stagnant society observing rather than shaping the fate of mankind.

Unsatisfied demand

The second reason is immediate and concrete: to meet an unsatisfied demand for higher education. Assuming that all young people with two A levels are qualified to undertake university work, the proportion of those who secured places in universities was approximately 65 per cent in 1966. This is no measure of the unsatisfied demand in many areas of study. For example, in 1967 3,667 students applied to read for a combined honours degree in arts in a university known to me. The university established a quota of 85 for entry and admitted 103. Assuming that all the 3,667 had applied to five other universities and all five admitted as many as this university, only one in six was able to enter. Nearly similar stories can be told of the social sciences and a large number of the natural sciences. The only sector in which demand is being approximately satisfied is to be found in some branches of technology.

The reasons for this volume of demand can be recapitulated briefly. More and more young people and their parents recognise that career prospects are becoming increasingly linked with the possession of degrees. There is an element of fashion and purposeless imitation in this attitude, but behind the trend is the increasingly evident need of industry, commerce, the arts, the sciences, administration and public life for men and women who have been trained to find their way into the vast complexity of accumulating knowledge and technique and to use them in the process of living. A degree is simply a sign which enables the work organisations of society to recognise quickly that a young person has undergone training and that there is a reasonable chance that, having been so educated, he or she will be able to contribute something positive to the activity of the organisation. Since the inception of universities in the twelfth century, entrants have been predominantly interested in careers. The organisations employing them have taken them because in the university they acquired knowledge of religion or law or science or literature or technology. The acquisition of a humane understanding and a cultivated sensibility is, and always has been, a side effect of university education, as it is of all disciplined mental effort. To consider humane understanding and the cultivation of sensibility as the main purposes of university education with a view to denying its vocational and practical value in civilised living is a perverse aspect of decadence, and is based on a false view of human experience and of the consequence of educative effort.

Britain has been a comparative latecomer in recognising that the function of universities is much broader than the creation of gentlemen and the supply of educated people to the traditional professions, to the higher public services and to pure scientific research. The British community is, too, a late developer in recognising in industrial and commercial activity, teaching and the public service the need for large numbers of people who are educated to use knowledge in their work and have the self-confidence and judgement which come from knowing what they are doing. The notion 'theirs not to reason why, theirs but to do as they are told' is no longer an adequate foundation for any organisation.

Hence the change in the demand both for higher education and for graduates; and the demand is bound to grow and cannot be arrested unless Britain wishes to drop out of modern life.

But can this demand for higher education be met? The universities are not meeting the demand. There exists what Mr Anthony Crosland, a former Minister of Education, has described as the public sector of higher education: the teachers' training colleges, the polytechnics, the colleges of commerce and technology and colleges of further education, all of which are equipped to provide degrees through the external examinations of the University of London or of the National Council of Academic Awards. But these agencies are insufficient. A recent report suggests that about 11 per cent of those who qualified for university but who did not get places went on to degree work outside universities. Besides being unable to meet demand, these specialised institutions are too heavily oriented towards training for one profession, such as elementary school teaching, to serve completely as institutions of higher education. Having a non-university status, they imply something less than university education, and are therefore not considered as desirable as universities in career terms. Whether there is any substance in this attitude is beside the point. The attitude exists, and the attempt on the part of the public authorities to maintain a status barrier in higher education is a real impairment of its effectiveness.

Britain is not alone as a community which cannot satisfy the demand for higher education. In the United States, Canada and Japan, where universities have achieved extremely high growth rates, the demand is still unsatisfied. The State of New York is now planning a state university to take more students than there are at present in all the universities of Great Britain, and this on the top of private institutions like Columbia University with 20,000 students, Cornell with 30,000 and New York University with 41,000. In Britain, on the other hand, the growth rate, rapid as it is in comparison with growth before 1950, is very slow. This is attributable to a number of influences, but principally to two: adherence to traditional conceptions of universities as élite institutions for the education of a very small proportion of the population, and dependence on the state as the main source of finance.

The determination to maintain the highest standards of instruction and achievement through all parts of all the universities has meant that they must necessarily remain small with high costs of production. These high costs have been borne, up to about 95 per cent, by the state. At the same time the state has extended its expenditure in a variety of other directions. Naturally there has been competition for scarce resources, because even in Britain there are limits to the extent to which the government can levy taxes. *The interposition of the University Grants Committee and the state between the universities and their customers has created a situation in which the universities cannot meet demand and tap directly the resources for satisfying it.* In order to get resources they have to compete with other tax-financed activities like the armed forces, the health services, the welfare programmes, the investment in public services, and so on. They have not put themselves in the position of competing for resources with the motor-car manufacturers, the breweries, the electronics industry, and so on.

There is absolutely no evidence that the British people will not spend more on higher education or that the state is obliged to finance universities because the people will not do it for themselves. Nor is there any evidence that young people from the lower income groups cannot find places in a free and independent university system. There are real psychological, moral and political limits to what the state can provide, and these limits are narrower than those that determine what people will provide for themselves in the presence of a felt need like that for food, prestige and opportunities for children. In spite of this the universities have preferred the position of pensioners of the state to that of free enterprises, with the natural result that they cannot respond directly to community demand. They are afraid to stimulate that demand and they do not know how to organise themselves to reap the rewards of so doing.

The vast majority of men and women in university life are no different from those in other walks of life in the motives that move them. They are as interested in money, prestige, promotion, opportunities and security as any other group of people. They compete for resources as much as businessmen, and when resources are scarce they are as fierce and as conservative as any other breed. If their considerable intelligence and energy were spent directly in satisfying the demand for higher education and in inventing ways of selling their products to an ever-widening body of consumers, they would serve society much more effectively than they do at present by fierce struggles to influence the government through the University Grants Committee to give them a larger share of the limited resources of the state. University vice-chancellors and the University Grants Committee believe they are interested in education because they fight for a place at the public feeding-trough on behalf of their own institutions. In effect their concern with higher education is directed to the preservation of the *status quo* in higher education. Consumer demand is a very secondary consideration, and this is bound to be so under the present method of financing the universities. More than one vice-chancellor has gone on strike over the preservation of the staff–student ratio in just the same way as shipwrights have done in the interest of the sanctity of a traditional job rendered obsolete by technological change and community need.

Response to the market

To the plain undeniable truth that the demand for higher education is not being met there can be added a third reason for starting an independent university: the need for different and better methods and purposes for higher education. As agencies of achieving intellectual excellence and providing the atmosphere for the discovery of knowledge on the farthest frontiers of many fields of inquiry, the British universities have compared favourably with the best of the great nations of the world. They can be given very high marks for the advancement of knowledge and the cultivation of sensibility. In the pursuit of these achievements they have taken small numbers of well-grounded young people of high ability and subjected them to rigorous courses which have come to be known as honours work. As discovery on the frontiers of knowledge has become more and more specialised, the universities have increasingly specialised their courses, and have exported specialisation to the schools, so that now young people are increasingly obliged to define their intellectual interests and to make major decisions very important in their future careers as early as fourteen or fifteen years of age, and often just at the moment when their minds are beginning to open out and delight in the broad variety of knowledge and experience. What was once a means of laying the foundation for brilliant achievement is now turning into its opposite and becoming an agency of intellectual narrowness and, worse, of boredom and disgust with learning.

For the very ablest young people premature specialisation is not harmful, because they tend to educate themselves broadly through their high level of awareness of the universe and of their capacity to analyse it. But for the vastly larger number of young people of good average intellectual ability, high specialisation narrows their intellect, and renders them useful to society and reconciled to themselves only if they find the slots in the adult world where their specialised techniques are of value. Much, if not all, honours degree work is designed on the assumption that every undergraduate participating is being fitted to work on the frontier of knowledge, and that, for those who do not, the experience of being so educated develops habits of mind which enable them to cope with the world and themselves. There is something in this argument, but not as much as is widely assumed. In practice a high percentage of the growing body of undergraduates go into business life, administration, the creative arts and elementary and secondary teaching not broadly and humanely educated but acquainted only with the jargon and techniques of narrow specialists. They are masters of the higher illiteracy, able to live with themselves and serve society only because three years of intellectual effort, even in specialised fields irrelevant to their real life, are better than no intellectual cultivation at all.

The honours system in higher education is an indispensable feature but it should not be the universal pattern of higher education. Higher education which aims at breadth of knowledge and awareness and the development of skill and sensitivity useful and necessary in the average, daily life of the world is not incompatible with intellectual excellence and the stretching of the mental and imaginative powers of young people. Broad education with utilitarian objectives need not be a soft option. Indeed, high specialisation is often a soft option representing an escape from the need to face the world and society and to contend with the confusions of human experience.

There is a place in the system of higher education for under-graduate programmes which aim at general education in the humanities and the sciences *together* and which have practical objectives such as the development of skill in the use of language, the use of electronic aids to thinking such as computers, and the capacity to understand and appreciate works of the imagination. The traditional honours programmes aim at producing discoverers of new knowledge. New programmes with a general education in view will produce *users* of new knowledge: not gentlemanly consumers of culture but people who in their daily lives as businessmen, administrators and teachers buy, interpret and apply new knowledge. As users their creative part in society consists in organising, transmitting and making available to the whole community what the pure scientist, the inspired artists and original technologists have produced. The notion that there is something second-rate and derivative in this role in society is nonsense. Many of Britain's difficulties stem from the poor quality and inadequate education of the administrators, organisers and transmitters of knowledge who are not equal to bringing to bear in the practical context of life the achievements of the élite of pure science and the arts. In general what is missing in Britain is *general* higher education because there is a serious failure, first, to recognise the importance of having large numbers so educated and, secondly, to recognise the inherent difficulty of such education.

There is a place in Britain for at least one university which is prepared to say what its students need to study in order to prepare themselves for a creative and responsible place in the modern world: to be governed in designing its programmes by the demands of society and not by the demands of discovery on the frontiers of knowledge. Without attempting to be specific in this matter it is possible to identify the areas in which teaching is required. First, there is education in the use of languages as a means of communication and not merely as a means of studying literature: the ways in which language is used in modern means of communication and the development of skill and precision in its use. Second, there is the development of understanding and appreciation of the imaginative works in literature, the fine arts, architecture and music. Third, the teaching of numerical methods so that quantitative relationships can be understood and computers deployed. Fourth, there is the need to understand the methods and principles of the natural sciences and technology so that the student can grasp sympathetically what scientists and technologists are doing and how they are doing it. Finally, there is the need to understand what the social scientists are doing and the relationship of the social sciences to the life of society.

A big programme? Yes. Most academics will dismiss such a programme as impossible – one that can at best be superficial and almost inevitably misleading. In order to see how this can be done we must turn from the academics to the journalists to see how they transmit the complicated and difficult to the uninformed or partially informed. A high level of understanding joined with a will to study methods of communication can solve this problem. The solution is more challenging than 85 per cent of the problems with which contemporary academics wrestle. And that problem is critical for our culture, our social efficiency, for the creative interchange of ideas and for the cultivation of sensibility.

Variety

There flows from the foregoing a fourth reason for establishing an independent university: the need to preserve and strengthen variety in English education. One of the great but unappreciated strengths of English education as a whole is the variety and individuality which it manages to cultivate, largely through the independence of its schools and its teachers and the absence of centralised systems of curricula design and control. The growth of state financing and control in all branches of education has not yet destroyed that variety but it can do so. We have only to look at what is happening to the universities to grasp the dangers.

The universities are now being engulfed in the long and general trend in British society which entrenches the past, slows down innovation and destroys individual initiative and responsibility; the growth of bureaucratic state control; the impairment of the state as leader and the development of the state as housekeeper and administrator; the universalising of the committee system so that everyone can refer everything to everyone else. Very few people in the British community have ever seriously doubted that an important foundation of the excellence of the universities is their independence; nor do many today. They have been very little the subject of the 'class struggle' arguments which have provided the ideological energy for transferring business enterprise to state ownership or control. Nonetheless they are being taken over by the state. Men like Sir Eric Ashby can produce an abundance of argument[1] to prove that the universities as pensioners of the state are really free and independent. What he cannot deny, however, is the

---

1   E.g. his Birkbeck College Foundation Oration, reported in *The Times*, 20 January 1968.

existence of control through financial provision, and that this control through the University Grants Committee, to which is now added the direct participation of the Ministry of Education and Science, has been the means of making a series of damaging mistakes the cumulative effects of which make it impossible for the universities to respond to the demand for higher education and almost impossible for them to change the direction of their efforts.

Let us be specific about the fundamental mistakes and the consequences now emerging. The University Grants Committee is responsible for the policy of building cottage universities – expensive to build, expensive to operate and ill designed to concentrate talent and variety of endeavour, which are indispensable to high academic achievement. Having created a high-cost system almost totally dependent on the state, the University Grants Committee and the Ministry of Education and Science are now faced with a crisis. How can the costs be met? The Minister of Education decrees sharply differential fees for foreign students. The University Grants Committee decides to expand the arts and the social sciences because they are for the time being low-cost faculties, and to expand them in the new cottage universities. What the effects of these decisions may be on the character and balance of the universities are now very much secondary to the overriding economic necessities generated by the original errors of the University Grants Committee. An important further consequence is the fear that the pressure to meet the demand for the education of undergraduates and the need to do so in low-cost faculties will have a prejudicial effect upon postgraduate work, particularly in the older institutions of international repute. Given the mistakes of the past it is now quite possible that limited resources will be spread so thinly that Britain may cease to possess university institutions of world class.

The decision-makers in the University Grants Committee, the Ministry of Education and Science and the Treasury are not insensitive men, but they are making purblind decisions because they are part of an elephantine system of centralised control. This foolishness is bound to grow, and is bound to engulf more and more university activity in the cobwebs of committee decisions primarily concerned with the system itself and only secondarily with the problem of education and of research.

The role of an independent university will be to do something different in higher education in terms both of the education provided and of organisation and response to community requirements. If an independent university is able to demonstrate that it can achieve an effective response from the community, it will show the existing universities the way back to independence and, perhaps, encourage some of them to see that they need not rely too heavily on the state for money and can hence have moral and practical claims to independent decision-making.

The case for the independence of universities hardly requires emphasis. There is one aspect of it, however, which has not been sufficiently considered. In the absence of an independent responsibility for its own existence, how can we tell whether a university is any good or not? The real test is whether or not students want to enter it and how much they and their parents are willing to sacrifice in the effort to do so. At the moment some universities are probably better than other universities, but there is no means of knowing. No university has an incentive to attract students and no successful university has the opportunity of building on its successes. If every university had to stand on its own feet, there would be no need for the Auditor General to crawl around the premises seeing how the money is being spent while assuring everyone that he is not interested in policy. The only reasons for interesting one-self in the spending of money are policy and purpose. If every university were independent and obliged to live by the judgement of the community expressed in terms of the use made of its service, there would be no need for the prolonged, complicated, bitter and wholly unnecessary quarrel over the division of scarce resources. The energy spent on debate and intrigue and developing the right connections would be spent on meeting the public demand.

Ways and means

How can a private university be started? How can one be maintained? How can it be made to grow?

The potential market

Only if there is a sufficiently strong-felt demand can such a university flourish. From the students' point of view any university in the state system is a low-cost university, and an independent university financed by charging the full cost of its services is bound to be a high-cost university. Other things being equal, nearly all students who can gain admission to the state-supported system will continue to prefer the existing universities. This leaves to the private university all the students who cannot find places, i.e. between 30 and 45 per cent of those who get two A levels, a group of some 25,000 or more. To these potential customers of a private university there must be added an undetermined number of predominantly young people who have not got two A levels for one reason or another, but whom aptitude tests reveal are equal to university work. There are another undetermined number of foreign students for whom the fees in existing universities are not so far out of line with those a private university will be obliged to charge. In the category of foreign students there are also the growing number of North American students wishing and being encouraged by their universities to spend one year in universities abroad. Finally, there are a further undetermined number, inevitably very small at first, who may prefer the programme of a private university to that of existing universities and are prepared to pay for this preference. Only careful market research can determine with some measure of certainty the size of this potential student body and its disposition and capacity to finance its own education.

An additional element of some importance is the existence of approximately 200,000 parents in Britain who are willing and able to pay for their children's education in fee-paying schools. Whether this body can be persuaded to add to their expenditure on education by financing three years at a university[2] or to give priority to university rather than primary or secondary education is another matter which requires careful investigation by market research.

Cost – and payment

The cost of attending a private university will be of the order of £1,500 a year for fees and moderate maintenance. It will be at once argued that no students – or very few – can spend £4,500 on a university education. How do we know? Since World War II, no one

---

2   Methods of pre-payment of fees by life assurance (with assistance of income tax rebates) and 'post-payment' by species of hire purchase have been developed in recent years and might be further expanded if the demand for financial assistance with university fees increased.

has even attempted to provide education on this basis. Let us assume that no student whose parents earn £1,500 or less can or will provide anything to finance the university education of a son or a daughter. Suppose, however, a hire-purchase system is worked out to permit payment over ten years, and this hire-purchase system is based on a non-profit revolving fund charging interest only sufficient to cover bad debts, rising price levels and to act as an incentive to repayment. Total cost to a student would be of the order of £5,500. It is known that university education increases earning capacity[3] and that this increase is larger for students from low-income groups. Suppose over a working life of 40 years a student improved his earning capacity by an average of only £500 a year or £20,000 in all; £20,000 on an outlay of £5,500 is not a bad return on money. In most cases the return will be much larger than the minimum here supposed.

In order further to assist student finances a private university must so organise its service workforce that part-time employment at commercial rates is open to students. The highly motivated student will welcome such opportunities, and the presence of the student honourably working to finance his education is something needed to create the serious sense of purpose which should underlie all higher education. Britain is no longer a master-and-servant society, and the sooner these dead stereotypes are banished from universities the better. Student employment opportunities will serve a moral as well as a financial purpose.

3 This subject has been studied by, *inter alia*, Professor G. S. Becker (1965), *Human Capital: A Theoretical and Empirical Analysis with Special Reference to Education*, National Bureau of Economic Research and Columbia University Press, New York; Professor Mark Blaug, 'The Rate of Return on Investment in Education in Great Britain', *Manchester School*, September 1965, and 'Approaches to Educational Planning', *Economic Journal*, June 1967.

The financial obstacles to developing a private university are largely illusory, provided that the university can offer programmes of study of a kind which will induce large numbers to invest comparatively large sums in the education provided. These provisos are critical for two reasons. Only large numbers will enable the institution to achieve economies of scale and only high fees will enable the university to grow to maturity and maintain its independence. Both these reasons require expansion.

Large numbers of students

At present in British universities the academic members of the university divide their time unevenly among three activities: teaching (usually in small groups), research and learning, and administration and policy-making concerning their own affairs. A small number additionally engage in consultative work or public service outside their university. The pattern varies with individuals on account of taste, talent or age, but that is how the total time of academics is spent. One result of this pattern of activities is a staff–student ratio which is high compared with universities on the continent of Europe and elsewhere in the English-speaking world. Inasmuch as salaries are a considerable component of university costs, unit costs in British universities are high. It is, of course, argued that British universities do in three years what other universities do in four or five years. There is something in this argument, but less than is generally supposed. The work in British sixth forms lasts at least two years, and British first degrees are achieved no younger on average than first degrees elsewhere.

Teaching on the one hand and research and learning on the other are indispensably linked together. One certainly cannot teach in a university without at the same time learning and researching, and it can be argued that research without teaching is undesirable and in some areas impossible. There is really no way round the problem of the university man doing two jobs: teaching and research. On the other hand, university administration and politics consume the time of academics. Many advances have been made in making university administration a specialised, professional activity, but nonetheless academics, and particularly the more highly paid, still spend much time in administration, and for a minority it is a prestige occupation which is preferred to teaching and learning. Outside consultation and public service work are valuable to a university and must be encouraged, provided the university is not converted into a salary-paying machine for people working elsewhere.

This pattern of academic work needs to be borne in mind in considering a 'unit cost-reducing' form of organisation. The teaching-learning combination cannot be altered, but it can be rearranged. If teaching activity can be intensified and professionalised, individual teachers can handle more students. Intensification can be achieved by so arranging activities that the teaching effort is not mixed up with the research and learning effort. In existing universities the academic staff are doing neither one nor the other to full effect because their activities are confused in time. Academic experience points to the fact that most learning and research is accomplished during vacations and during leave of absence, and it is then that real intellectual refreshment is achieved. Teaching depletes energy and intellectual resources, and the attempt to mix research and teaching weakens both activities. Too often academics just do not learn to teach, and succeed in confusing the students and wasting their time.

If a new university recognised that teaching is the main activity at one period of time and learning and research at another, and if staff are chosen *and trained* to teach, there will be a large increase in productivity. The staff–student ratio is at the root of high unit costs, but it does not follow that a low staff–student ratio means neglect of students or exploitation of staff. On the contrary, a private university must seek staff with two known capacities: intellectual capacity and capacity to teach or capacity to learn to teach. Accordingly, individual staff members of a private university will have to be paid considerably more than the staff of existing universities, and they will have to be given at least one year in six of paid leave for intellectual refreshment and the uninterrupted pursuit of intellectual inquiry.

In return for more pay and guaranteed and long periods of free time, the staff member will be asked to have his energies and abilities as a teacher deployed in such a way that large numbers can be handled. Enrolment in each year in a viable private university will have to be at least 3,500. Mass education – the horror of it! Not at all. Modern media of communication will enable a small number of brilliant teachers to reach more students more often than any do at present. At some time those teachers with a capacity for (and training in) face-to-face instruction in small groups will be able to handle more students and stimulate more response if they teach 25 hours a week during terms.

Hand in hand there must be developed a new conception of academic liberty – not necessarily the best or the only conception of academic liberty, but one required for university independence. The idea of a university post as a freehold until 65 to 67 to be followed by a life pension must be abandoned. In its place we must develop the conception of university teaching as a skilled profession with a commitment to the policies of the institution which in turn are determined by the relationship of the institution with the surrounding society. Put briefly, it will be necessary to develop in the university a business conception of duty in place of the aristocratic and rentier conception of duty. In a private university the teacher's liberty will consist in being able to take it or leave it and having the economic means to do so; but not in the liberty to impose his conception of his duty on the organisation. There are many virtues in existing conceptions of academic liberty, but there are many drawbacks too. There is a place and a need for an alternative concept to meet the requirements of university teachers willing to settle for something more than security and the entrenchment of their own interests at the expense of institutional mobility and capacity for quick response to social need and the generation of new knowledge.

High fees

The need for high university fees is obvious, but we must define what 'high' means and explain the reason for high fees. Fees will inevitably be high compared with those of existing universities because the full cost of operation of a private university must come from the sale of its services – both of teaching and research. The contribution of fees to the cost of existing universities is of the order of 5–10 per cent. Fees paying full cost will necessarily be high by comparison, but they must also be high in relation to unit costs in order to provide the capital for growth both in numbers of students and in the variety and quality of services rendered. Good orchestras, good art galleries, good theatres and good research institutions are indispensable to a good university. They can only be justified and paid for if their cost is widely spread. If large-scale operation is achieved the gap between high fees and low unit costs can be narrowed, but without the investment made possible by high fees value for money cannot be achieved.

Four steps

To establish an independent university, four steps must be taken.

i) The market

The first essential step is to determine whether there exists in Britain and the world at large a market for the services such a university can provide, i.e. for broadly based general education aimed at the development of the skill and understanding required to make a positive contribution to an advanced society. If the market is not there or is not big enough, the project cannot be launched.

ii) The charter

If the answer to the first question is positive, the sponsors of the independent university must secure a charter from the Privy Council. Nothing in the laws of the United Kingdom requires it, but the nature and structure of British society do. Many employers, particularly those organised as professions, will recognise and many can legally recognise only the degrees of a chartered institution. Although the true charter of any university is the quality of its staff and students, an independent university must have the official endorsement which a charter implies. To this end the sponsors must be men and women of good repute as academics and as citizens, and the programmes of teaching and learning proposed must command the approval of people of understanding and goodwill.

(iii) The capital

The next step will be to secure the capital necessary for land, buildings and an educational hire-purchase revolving fund. About £5 million will be needed. A private university need not refuse outright gifts, but its financial policies should be so designed that its capital costs and depreciation, as well as running costs, are supported from revenue derived from fees and research contracts. To start it will require something that clearly resembles gifts, but in principle there is no reason why the foundation funds should not be repayable over, say, 50 years, should not bear interest and should not be secured on land and buildings. To suppose otherwise is to pander to the false notion that education is a special kind of activity dependent on charitable impulses or state subsidies. This is particularly not true of higher education. One of the basic emotional factors in higher education is a realisation on the part of the students and their parents that what they are undertaking is significant and important for themselves and society and that the effort made to carry out a programme of education has both its cost and its rewards. No matter what the rewards may be, the costs are inevitable, and it cannot but be socially healthy for people to make their choices with some measurable conception of what they are doing.

(iv) Programme of study

If the initial capital can be raised or is reasonably in prospect, the fourth step is to plan in detail the programmes of study. All decisions on buildings, staffing and admissions policy will depend upon the chosen programmes of teaching. This will be the most difficult step to take, for the good reason that it is a step into the unknown, If the programmes are simply borrowings from and/or simplifications of existing university courses, the institution will fail. The plain truth is that a new independent university will have to turn out better-educated people from students who the existing universities have turned down or failed to attract. This can be done by using programmes capable of heightening intellectual interest and intensifying motivation and by using teaching methods which combine intellectual stimulation with the careful development of skill. To achieve such ends both research and imagination of a high order and a new kind will be required. The people to do this need not be numerous but they must be brilliant, inventive and bold: who know what they are doing and who love what they know.

There is no formula for an instant university. An independent university in the British context will necessarily be a very specialised institution in relation to the kind of students it attracts and the kind of education it provides. It can and must become soon after its full establishment a mature university in its provision for a high level of honours work in a limited number of faculties and studies and graduate work in them. No university, if it intends to be good, can rely only on high-quality staff. It must attract some high-quality students who want from the start to do specialised work. That such students are necessarily limited in number (as is true in existing universities) will be recognised as a desideratum in the proposed university, and high-cost programmes will be provided when the quality of the student justifies the cost.

In designing its programmes an independent university must

fix goals. Its minimum goals in education must be a degree which means its holder can read English, and write it accurately and felicitously, and use English as a means of communicating with large numbers and as a means of communicating complex information. Existing universities assume students have this capacity, but the assumption is not always true when students enter the universities nor when they leave them. It must aim at developing this power in a foreign language. For English people foreign languages are no longer a matter of taste and inclination. They are a necessity for everyone aspiring to play any directive or creative role in society. They can be taught to all except a small minority of the 'language blind'. And all must be taught the elementary techniques of data processing and data analysis by computers.

Some young people come to universities with some of these skills developed, but the specialisation imposed on schools by the honours system in universities ensures that none have all of them. In an independent university existing skill will be honed finer and new skill developed so that the student has a basic armoury of weapons for survival in international, technological society.

On the basis of these skills the humanities and the sciences can be taught together. The assumption on which the minimum goals rest is simply what experience and common sense suggest: that a person who speaks French is more likely to understand Pascal or Sartre or the politics of the Fifth Republic than one who does not; that a person who can design an elementary computer programme and recognise a significant correlation is more likely to learn some economics or understand an engineering problem than one who cannot; and that one who can read a book and write exact English is more likely to be able to appreciate John Donne or Iris Murdoch or write a report than one who cannot.

The maximum goals of the programme must be to ensure that the graduate is capable of finding his way into any body of knowledge: not to do what the specialist does but to understand what he does, and its relevance to society; to have some feeling for the interrelationship of the sciences and of the arts.

Admissions

To achieve these goals the programme must be designed in sequence so that the students move from skill to broad experience to study in depth. Such a programme should aim at making all graduates capable of doing useful work in responsible jobs, and ensuring that at least half are intellectually as able as the first- and second-class honours graduates of existing universities.

Such a programme requires a carefully designed admissions policy. There is no need to assume that existing A-level examinations constitute the sole test of capacity to undertake university education. On the other hand a university which demands from students high fees must be prepared to discover as accurately as possible whether applicants are able to undertake the work required. Selection procedures will necessarily have to be more carefully designed than those of existing universities, and better calculated to discover potential for education than capacity for undergoing written examinations.

Conclusion

There seems to be an accumulating body of evidence that British society is not performing as well as its past history and its present opportunities would suggest it can perform. Whether there is any significance or truth in this evidence is difficult to say, but the impression of *malaise* is there and affects attitudes and confidence. Our socio-economic and political organisation seems to have become over-elaborate and constipated. The larger purpose of this proposal to establish an independent university is to see whether there is some way out of our situation by the decentralisation of decision-making and by the creation of centres of individual and institutional decision-making which involve the individual and/or the institution responding directly to the general environment rather than indirectly under the guidance of agencies that seem to understand even less about the problems of response than the individual or the institution itself. If all knowledge is limited and uncertain, and all human beings and agencies make mistakes in their life strategy, the question is simply what arrangement will minimise the mistakes and maximise correct solutions. In the present circumstances an arrangement that encourages individuals and institutions to plan their own strategies seems on balance to have a prospect of more success than centralised, overall planning. And such an arrangement does impart excitement to life, which is not an unconsidered trifle.

Assuming that this larger purpose of establishing an independent university is valid in the present circumstances of British society, the problem is to find a practical means for its realisation. It must be recognised that the goal of an independent centre of excellence in teaching and learning can be achieved only in stages; that it can come into being only by doing what existing universities either cannot do or do not wish to do; that what it does must be done on a large scale in order to command the resources necessary to extend the scope and character of its work; that it will produce quality only by learning how to work with quantity; and that, finally, it will be no easy task to achieve the standards of the best teachers and students in existing British universities.

Appendix
The urgency of an independent university

Disquiet among academics about the threat to the independence of university scholarship from growing political influence is not of recent origin. Recurrent concern by a number of economists associated with the IEA found expression during 1968 in two small conferences at which a paper by Professor H. S. Ferns of Birmingham University was considered by senior academics, including Professor Max Beloff, Sir Sydney Caine, Dr R. B. McCallum, Colin Clark, Professor Mark Blaug, Professor Ernst Chain and Professor Charles Wilson.

This paper, *Towards an Independent University*, is published on 8 January 1969 to coincide with a third private conference in London where finance, syllabus, admissions and other practical problems will be further examined. Meanwhile a Declaration on the urgency of establishing an independent university (reproduced below) was circulated among a short list of academics, mainly in economics faculties, to gauge the likely degree of support from among the kind of teachers and administrators who would staff such a pioneering institution.

Of the 46 distinguished educationists who have put their names to this Declaration in a personal capacity, some have reservations on specific propositions but all have expressed unqualified support for the general principle. Others expressed support but withheld their signatures because of professional embarrassment, doubts about raising funds or fears that an independent university might be too successful in raising funds at the expense of private subsidies to existing institutions of higher education. Finally, some could not indicate adherence owing to absence abroad.

Declaration

1. The euphoria in British universities following the Robbins Report is fading. Despite a period of rapid expansion of existing universities and the proliferation of new ones, Britain still lags behind other wealthy societies in the provision of university education for graduates and postgraduates and suffers from a damaging brain-drain of graduates of the highest attainment. The process of expansion itself has been hindered and planning made more difficult by stop-go in public finance. Student discontent – and staff discontent – reveals a continuing malaise.

2. We believe that the machinery for relating the state and state finance to the universities has become clumsy and wasteful and leads to increasingly resented measures of detailed control which handicap experiment and innovation. Even Oxford and Cambridge do not command sufficient independent income to be immune from this process.

3. We believe that independence in scholarship, learning and research cannot flourish if all universities are financed from one dominant source, governmental or private, and that the only way to multiply and diversify the sources of finance is to look to private individuals, industry and trusts.

4. We believe that the most potent challenge to the financial, ad-

ministrative and educational assumptions of the existing system is the creation of new institutions dependent upon private endowments, gifts, students' fees and service income. Such institutions would be obliged to make better use of equipment and students' and teachers' time and to base their policies upon an assessment of the changing market for graduates and research.

5. We consider that a new approach to syllabus and teaching methods would enable an independent university to develop its own forms of excellence which could rival the best in the existing system.

6. We believe that an independent university could find and attract students without difficulty in what is likely to be a continuing shortage of university places, and could help improve the quality of the intake by looking for more mature students whose motivation to work and achievement is strong, and whose capacity for self-discipline has been enhanced by experience of gainful employment.

7. We see powerful economic, social and political arguments for enabling students who so wish to finance themselves with the help of loans, rather than leaving them wholly or substantially dependent on governmental funds. We believe that student unrest and demands for democracy are aggravated by the virtually complete dependence of both staff and students on public subvention.

8. We believe that fuller scope and incentive for contract research for governmental and private institutions and firms, possibly in

association with teaching, could lead to a more fruitful inter-relationship between the university and industrial and social life as is common in the United States.

9. We believe that such a university, by freedom in methods and scale of remuneration and charges, could attract staff and students from outside Britain and strengthen the influence of British scholarship in the international community.

10. We acknowledge that such a university would require a massive infusion of funds to compete in quality with existing state-supported and politically controlled British universities, but we believe that its endowment would be more attractive to industry and the foundations than grants to existing institutions where the result of private generosity is a mild relief to the Exchequer, and where state control threatens to prevent it being put to full use in novel or experimental purposes.

December 1968

Signatories
PROFESSOR H. B. ACTON
University of Edinburgh

G. C. ALLEN
Emeritus Professor, University of London

W. A. BARKER
Headmaster, The Leys School, Cambridge

DR W. H. S. BARNES
Vice-Chancellor, University of Liverpool

PROFESSOR MAX BELOFF
University of Oxford

PROFESSOR MARK BLAUG
University of London

PROFESSOR M. L. BURSTEIN
Universities of California (Santa Barbara) and Warwick

THE LORD CACCIA
Provost, Eton College

SIR SYDNEY CAINE
Formerly Director, LSE

COLIN CLARK
University of Oxford

M. W. CRANSTON
Professor-Elect, University of London

PROFESSOR D. R. DENMAN
University of Cambridge

PROFESSOR G. A. DUNCAN
Pro-Chancellor, University of Dublin

PROFESSOR H. S. FERNS
University of Birmingham

PROFESSOR S. H. FRANKEL
University of Oxford

PROFESSOR NORMAN GASH
Vice-Principal, University of St Andrews

PROFESSOR N. J. GIBSON
New University of Ulster

PROFESSOR D. C. HAGUE
University of Manchester

PROFESSOR T. W. HUTCHISON
University of Birmingham

DR R. L. JAMES
Headmaster, Harrow School

PROFESSOR ELLIOTT JAQUES
Brunel University

PROFESSOR JOHN JEWKES
University of Oxford

PROFESSOR H. G. JOHNSON
London School of Economics and University of Chicago

DR W. LETWIN
London School of Economics

PROFESSOR R. G. LIPSEY
University of Essex

PROFESSOR RICHARD LYNN
The Economic and Social Research Institute, Dublin

PROFESSOR D. G. MACRAE
London School of Economics

DR R. B. MCCALLUM
The Principal, St Catherine's, Windsor

M. W. MCCRUM
Headmaster, Tonbridge School

P. G. MASON
High Master, Manchester Grammar School

PROFESSOR E. V. MORGAN
University of Manchester

PROFESSOR M. J. OAKESHOTT
London School of Economics

F. W. PAISH
Emeritus Professor, University of London

PROFESSOR A. T. PEACOCK
Deputy Vice-Chancellor, University of York

PROFESSOR A. R. PREST
University of Manchester

PROFESSOR B. C. ROBERTS
London School of Economics

PROFESSOR W. M. SIMON
University of Keele

PROFESSOR JOHN VAIZEY
Brunel University

PROFESSOR A. A. WALTERS
London School of Economics

PROFESSOR J. W. N. WATKINS
London School of Economics

DR E. G. WEST
University of Kent

PROFESSOR CHARLES WILSON
University of Cambridge

PROFESSOR TOM WILSON
University of Glasgow

PROFESSOR JACK WISEMAN
University of York

PROFESSOR B. S. YAMEY
London School of Economics

PROFESSOR A. J. YOUNGSON
University of Edinburgh

ABOUT THE IEA

The Institute is a research and educational charity (No. CC 235 351), limited by guarantee. Its mission is to improve understanding of the fundamental institutions of a free society with particular reference to the role of markets in solving economic and social problems.

The IEA achieves its mission by:

- a high quality publishing programme
- conferences, seminars, lectures and other events
- outreach to school and college students
- brokering media introductions and appearances

The IEA, which was established in 1955 by the late Sir Antony Fisher, is an educational charity, not a political organisation. It is independent of any political party or group and does not carry on activities intended to affect support for any political party or candidate in any election or referendum, or at any other time. It is financed by sales of publications, conference fees and voluntary donations.

In addition to its main series of publications the IEA also publishes a quarterly journal, _Economic Affairs_, and has two specialist programmes – Environment and Technology, and Education.

The IEA is aided in its work by a distinguished international Academic Advisory Council and an eminent panel of Honorary Fellows. Together with other academics, they review prospective IEA publications, their comments being passed on anonymously to authors. All IEA papers are therefore subject to the same rigorous independent refereeing process as used by leading academic journals.

IEA publications enjoy widespread classroom use and course adoptions in schools and universities. They are also sold throughout the world and often translated/reprinted.

Since 1974 the IEA has helped to create a world-wide network of 100 similar institutions in over 70 countries. They are all independent but share the IEA's mission.

Views expressed in the IEA's publications are those of the authors, not those of the Institute (which has no corporate view), its Managing Trustees, Academic Advisory Council members or senior staff.

Members of the Institute's Academic Advisory Council, Honorary Fellows, Trustees and Staff are listed on the following page.

The Institute gratefully acknowledges financial support for its publications programme and other work from a generous benefaction by the late Alec and Beryl Warren.

295

For information about subscriptions to IEA publications, please contact:

Subscriptions
The Institute of Economic Affairs
2 Lord North Street
London SW1P 3LB

Tel: 020 7799 8900
Fax: 020 7799 2137
Website: www.iea.org.uk/books/subscribe.htm

Other papers recently published by the IEA include:

WHO, What and Why?

Transnational Government, Legitimacy and the World Health Organization
Roger Scruton
Occasional Paper 113
ISBN 0 255 36487 3

The World Turned Rightside Up

A New Trading Agenda for the Age of Globalisation
John C. Hulsman
Occasional Paper 114
ISBN 0 255 36495 4

The Representation of Business in English Literature

Introduced and edited by Arthur Pollard
Readings 53
ISBN 0 255 36491 1

Anti-Liberalism 2000

The Rise of New Millennium Collectivism
David Henderson
Occasional Paper 115
ISBN 0 255 36497 0

Capitalism, Morality and Markets

Brian Griffiths, Robert A. Sirico, Norman Barry and Frank Field
Readings 54
ISBN 0 255 36496 2

A Conversation with Harris and Seldon

Ralph Harris and Arthur Seldon
Occasional Paper 116
ISBN 0 255 36498 9

Malaria and the DDT Story

Richard Tren & Roger Bate
Occasional Paper 117
ISBN 0 255 36499 7

**A Plea to Economists Who Favour Liberty:
Assist the Everyman**

Daniel B. Klein
Occasional Paper 118
ISBN 0 255 36501 2

Waging the War of Ideas
John Blundell
Occasional Paper 119
ISBN 0 255 36500 4

The Changing Fortunes of Economic Liberalism
Yesterday, Today and Tomorrow
David Henderson
Occasional Paper 105 (new edition)
ISBN 0 255 36520 9

The Global Education Industry
Lessons from Private Education in Developing Countries
James Tooley
Hobart Paper 141 (new edition)
ISBN 0 255 36503 9

Saving Our Streams
The Role of the Anglers' Conservation Association in Protecting English and Welsh Rivers
Roger Bate
Research Monograph 53
ISBN 0 255 36494 6

Better Off Out?

The Benefits or Costs of EU Membership
Brian Hindley and Martin Howe
Occasional Paper 99 (new edition)
ISBN 0 255 36502 0

To order copies of currently available IEA papers, or to enquire about availability, please contact:

Lavis Marketing
73 Lime Walk
Oxford OX3 7AD

Tel: 01865 767575
Fax: 01865 750079
Email: orders@lavismarketing.co.uk